The Aethiopica • Heliodorus (of Emes. Society, Athens

Publisher's Note

The book descriptions we ask booksellers to display prominently warn that this is an historic book with numerous typos or missing text; it is not indexed or illustrated.

The book was created using optical character recognition software. The software is 99 percent accurate if the book is in good condition. However, we do understand that even one percent can be an annoying number of typos! And sometimes all or part of a page may be missing from our copy of the book. Or the paper may be so discolored from age that it is difficult to read. We apologize and gratefully acknowledge Google's assistance.

After we re-typeset and design a book, the page numbers change so the old index and table of contents no longer work. Therefore, we often remove them; otherwise, please ignore them.

Our books sell so few copies that you would have to pay hundreds of dollars to cover the cost of our proof reading and fixing the typos, missing text and index. Instead we let most customers download a free copy of the original typo-free scanned book. Simply enter the barcode number from the back cover of the paperback in the Free Book form at www.RareBooksClub.com. You may also qualify for a free trial membership in our book club to download up to four books for free. Simply enter the barcode number from the back cover onto the membership form on our home page. The book club entitles you to select from more than a million books at no additional charge. Simply enter the title or subject onto the search form to find the books.

If you have any questions, could you please be so kind as to consult our Frequently Asked Questions page at www.RareBooksClub.com/faqs.cfm? You are also welcome to contact us there.

General Books LLC™, Memphis, USA, 2012.

250 *Copies of this work have been privately printed on ordinary paper solely for distribution amongst the Members of the Athenian Society. None of these copies are for sale. 5 Special Copies have also been privately printed on Japanese Vellum. None of these copies are for sale. The Council of the Society pledge themselves never to reprint nor to re-issue in any form.* (THE AETHIOPICA)

LITERALLY AND COMPLETELY TRANSLATED FROM THE GREEK, WITH INTRODUCTION AND NOTES

ATHENS: PRIVATELY PRINTED FOR THE ATHENIAN SOCIETY: MDCCCXCVII

INTRODUCTION

It is not in the early literature of Greece and Rome that the romance of love and adventure must be looked for.1 We can observe the remote origin of writings of this kind during the Attic period, we can follow its obscure development in the Alexandrine period, but it is not until the Roman period that its growth and perfection become perceptible.

We must not be surprised at the tardy recognition accorded by the ancients to a class of literature which is so popular amongst ourselves — distinguished from history by the admixture of fiction and the comparative unimportance of the events described; from poetry by the employment of prose and the representation of the manners of social life in place of the nearly always ideal picture of life in general. The fact is to be 1 See Introduction to *Daphnis and Chloe.* explained by the difference of manners and societies.

Amongst the peoples of modern times, the progress of the sciences and abstract studies has somewhat dried up the sources of poetical fables, and the political constitution of the great states of Europe, even of those where the greatest liberty is allowed to each citizen, does not ... vate life. In Greece and Rome, on the contrary, it was not until late that the imagination was sated with the marvellous as introduced in the epic fables; and, as long as the turbulent freedom of the little Greek republics and the city of Rome occupied, in the Agora and in the Forum, the existence of nearly all the citizens, the picture of the ordinary circumstances of private life was capable of attracting, and at the same time, not strong enough, to retain its hold upon men's minds. Preference was given to the heroic spectacles of tragedy, and, in its first origin, even comedy itself only borrowed its interest from political passions. It was not until the time of Menander, that is to say, the period of the Macedonian conquest, that comedy became a picture of private life; and then it became possible for romance to make its appearance. No doubt the *Milesian Fables* may claim greater antiquity; but they were originally only simple oral recitals, like the *Phrygian Fables* or the Aesopian apologue, and they came into being in the midst of a society quite different from that of the other. Greek populations — a society in which the enjoyments of private life caused the interests of public life to be forgotten.

In Greek society, before the Macedonian conquest, and in Roman society, before the Empire, everything concurred in retarding the development of these pictures of familiar life. In fact, in the young days of their republics, the Greeks and Romans had scarcely any time to devote to reading simply for the sake of amusement; their whole life was taken up by private and public affairs; literature itself was an active and, in a manner, a living literature, which addressed itself to hearers rather than readers, and filled the temples, the theatres, the festivals, the law courts, and the schools.

In proportion as the activity of public life died out in Greece and Rome, the

taste for pictures of manners was bound to spread. Already, in Euripides, we see tragedy departing from its heroic traditions and manifesting a taste for romantic pictures of *bourgeois* life; in the *"Flower"* of Agathon, tragedy is nothing but a romance. The New Comedy sprang up under the successors of Alexander. It must be observed that, in the works of Menander, Alexis, and Philemon, the family sanctuary is not yet open, and that these poets limit themselves to describing courtesans, young men and women, fathers, and slaves. We may believe that, at the same period, the *Milesian Fables* made their way from Ionia to Greece, the authors of which, more audacious, no doubt cast indiscreet glances upon the interior of the household; but these fables were only short stories, very different from the lengthy narratives to which the Roman period gave birth. It is not until then that writers such as Petronius, Lucian, Apuleius, Iamblichus, Heliodorus, and Achilles Tatius appeared. A new era had also commenced for the ancient world; with the Empire, an end was put to republican manners and public life; excess of liberty had strangled liberty; there were no longer any citizens; private individuals had ample leisure, which they were able to occupy by frivolous reading, and the rhetoricians took advantage of the idleness of the wealthy classes to launch into their midst interminable romances of love and adventure.

The Kast is the true country of stories of this nature, because the East has been from all time the land of political slavery and private life. It is in the East that we find the oldest examples of compositions of this kind; it is in the Greek countries most exposed to contact with Oriental civilisation, that is to say, in Asia Minor, that the first attempts of romantic literature among the Greeks made their appearance, and it is there, above all, that later they find their development. Ionia has produced the *Milesian Fables;* Iamblichus, the author of the *Babylonica,* was born in Syria, as was Lucian, the author of *Lucius1* and the *True History;* Heliodorus came from Emesa in Phoenicia, Achilles Tatius from Alexandria. Cyprus, Antioch, and

1 This is not universally admitted.

Ephesus have given birth to three romance-writers each named Xenophon.

It is impossible to deny that the influence of Oriental fancy has inclined certain imaginations to the marvellous and extraordinary, and in this manner favoured, in Greece, the development of romantic compositions; but it seems less probable that the Greek Romance is the direct product of Oriental stories.1 The character of the Oriental stories and the Greek Romances is not, in general, the same. In spite of a number of somewhat unnatural and improbable pictures, the whole colouring of the latter is Greek, even to the pictures of Eastern life. The marvellous, which holds a certain place in some of these fabulous narratives, never exhibits the breadth and simplicity of the marvellous which is so predominant in the Eastern stories. The taste for romance has passed from the East into Greece, but romance has become transformed. We know how readily the Greek race assimilated and stamped with the impress of its genius all that it borrowed from foreign civilisations. The 1 As maintained by Huet, in his *Lettre à Segrais sur l'origine des romans.*

I

Greeks were naturally story-tellers; before fabulous narratives became, in the hands of the rhetoricians, a form of literature, they had told tales in abundance, in which the Eastern influence might have lost itself and disappeared. Such were the stories told by mothers and nurses to their children, by the idlers in the barbers' shops, by parasites and guests at banquets. Even in the highways of Athens there were to be found persons who made it their profession to relate stories for the amusement of the passersby, like *Philepsius* in the *Plutus* of Aristophanes.

These oral tales were of various kinds. There were moral tales, after the style of the Aesopian apologue, and the *Libyan Fable*; humorous and satirical tales, to which the *Sybaritic Fables* had given rise. In their origin, these fables, which were sometimes called the *Sybaritic Apophthegms,* were not so much stories as witty anecdotes and sayings, like those which Aristophanes (in the *Wasps)* puts into the mouth of Philocleon.

But it is doubtful whether the *Sybaritic Fables* always preserved their primitive simplicity, and the close alliance between Sybaris and Miletus seems in time to have confounded these stories with the *Milesian Fables.* We have mentioned the stories which had the greatest vogue amongst the ancients, both when they were still transmitted orally, and when, later, they were collected, altered, or imitated by various writers. But it was a far cry from these brief and fugitive stories to the long romances which were later composed by the rhetoricians.

Before we proceed to devote our attention to these romances, it is necessary to cast a rapid glance upon the stories which gave birth to them.

It was natural that the elegant and effeminate Ionia should be a centre of erotic tales. The very name of the Ionians recalls the people most happily gifted of all the Hellenes, the people in whose midst were very early developed poetry, philosophy, music, architecture— all the elegances and delicacies of civilisation, but also the people most inclined to the refinements of sensual pleasure.

Subject in turn to the rule of the Lydians and Persians, they had always been more anxious for comfort than for liberty, which in their opinion consisted in the absence of all restraint in their pleasures. A Sybarite remarked, "In all my travels I have only found one free city, Miletus." Miletus, the birthplace of Aspasia and so many courtesans, as famous as those of Corinth, afforded, in fact, the model of the kind of independence which won for it the admiration of the inhabitants of Sybaris and established friendly relations between the two cities. Miletus, like Sybaris, gave birth to a host of agreeable, but mostly licentious stories, which spread throughout Greece, together with the renown of these two cities, the taste for

their pleasures.

In vain was Miletus desolated by the Persian War; in vain was Sybaris destroyed; the *Milesian* and *Sybaritic Tales* succeeded to the prosperity of both. These tales formed the delight of degenerate Rome. After the defeat at Carrhae, a collection of stories of this kind was found amongst the baggage of a Roman officer, and the *Surena* read it to the Senate of Seleucia, to give them an idea of the manners of the arrogant people who claimed to be able to subjugate the Parthians.1 Albinus (the rival of 1 See *Plutarch,* Life of Crassus, ch. 32.
i

Septimius Severus), who was for some time Emperor, occupied the leisure which his ambition permitted him in reading Apuleius and composing Milesian Tales, which his courtiers considered excellent, but for which his historian professes only a moderate regard. 1

The most famous of the *Milesian Tales* was that which was composed (it is not known when) by a certain Aristides of Miletus and translated into Latin by Lucius Cornelius Sisenna. It is twice mentioned by Ovid, who seems to say that the work was presented in the form of a history. The work probably contained, together with a short sketch of Milesian history, various anecdotes of Milesian life. These anecdotes were Milesian Tales. Similar works had already been composed by a certain Hegesippus and some other writers, whom Parthenius of Nicaea mentions without naming. In the love-stories written by this grammarian, we find several Milesian tales, for we must, no doubt, regard as such, not only those which Parthenius borrowed from Hegesippus or some writer 1 See *Scriptorts Historiae Augustae,* Vita Albini, by Julius Capitolinus, ch. 11-12.

I of *Milesian Histories,* but also those of which the scene is laid at Miletus, and which have for their subject the incontinence of the women of this city. The memory of these tales lingers in all the erotic narratives of antiquity, especially the oldest. One of the interlocutors in Lucien's *Amores,* speaking of similar stories which he has just heard, calls them *Milesian Tales.* Apuleius merely strung together several stories of this kind, such as the history of the amorous step-mother, and the story of the "washing-tub," from which La Fontaine has borrowed.

It seems doubtful whether the fable of *Psyche* should be included, although purely imaginative fictions somewhat obliterate its originally allegorical character. The Milesian Tales gave more room to the senses than to sentiment. At most, there was intermingled some moral lesson, as in one of Parthenius's stories; or some satirical meaning, as in the *Ephesian Matron.* This last story, one of the incidental episodes of Petronius, no doubt also came to him from Ionia.

Perhaps Ephesus, like Miletus, had her erotic literature; in Xenophon she produced her Aristides. At any rate, like Miletus, this city was famous for its fondness for pleasure, and it is in one of the two that the Greek romance writers, as a rule, place the scene of their stories.

The Milesian Tales exhibit the first form of the erotic tales of antiquity. They were slight and hasty sketches, like the *Fabliaux* of the Middle Ages (only in prose) and the *Nouvelles* of Boccacio's *Decameron,* or the *Heptameron* of Marguerite of Navarre. Intended solely to amuse and excite sensual imaginations, they at first had no literary pretensions, and, being more natural, were the more agreeable. Perhaps, as a rule, they were not longer than the stories of the same kind which were extracted from various historians by Parthenius of Nicaea to furnish his friend Cornelius Gallus with subjects for elegy. We see from the work of Parthenius, from a similar collection of stories by Plutarch, from some of the *Narratives* of Conon, and the *Varia Historia* of Aelian, that the influence of the Milesian Tales made itself felt even in history, into which it introduced a number of erotic and, for the most part, imaginary episodes.

Such were the stories relating to Rhodopis the courtesan. According to some, she built one of the pyramids of Egypt by inviting each of her lovers to bring a stone; according to others, she became queen of Egypt thanks to the loss of her slipper, like Cinderella. The name of Rhodopis is as dear to the Greek romance-writers as that of Helen is to the poets. In *Theagenes and Chariclea,* the seductions of another Rhodopis nearly triumphed over the austerity of a high priest of Memphis; and in *Leucippe and Clitophon,* we meet with another Rhodopis, but this time so pure and virtuous as to provoke the wrath of the goddess of Love. Plutarch, in his *Moralia,* mentions, together with the Panthea of Xenophon, the Timoclea of Aristobulus and the Thebe of Theopompus. This list might be increased by the stories of this class which have been extracted from history by Conon, Parthenius, and Plutarch.

The Milesian Tale passed from history into the writings of philosophers. It has left its traces in the *Symposium* of Xenophon, the *Treatise upon Love* by Clearchus of Soli, some similar works ъ by Theophrastus, Ariston of Iulis, Sphodrius the Cynic, Favorinus of Aries, and some of the intermingled dialogues and stories which Plutarch has left us. It was not until considerably later (perhaps shortly before the time of Petronius) that the love-stories, so brief in the Milesian Fables, so rapid when they were intermingled with history and historical or philosophical romances, underwent extended developments. The ancient stories of the Milesian class were sometimes preserved, in the form of episodes, in the lengthy romances which came into being during the Roman and Byzantine periods; but, as a rule, they were lost in fuller and more extended narratives, which embraced a longer period of time and surrounded the principal incident and the chief characters with a number of secondary incidents and characters. The transition from the tale to the romance did not take place without an effort.

It is sufficient to compare the *Lucius* and the *Metamorphoses* of Apuleius to see how completely artificial was the method which combined a number of

episodic tales with the fable of romance, and how obvious the " soldering " was.

Few stones, in ancient times, met with as great success as the tale of Lucius transformed into an ass by a magic ointment, and afterwards restored to human form by eating roses. It was not only an erotic story, it was a tale of a fantastic character, which was highly popular in ancient days. While the poets fed the popular imagination with stories of the Olympian Gods and Goddesses, superstition continually multiplied tales of supernatural beings and marvellous occurrences. In order to make children good, they were told amusing fables, such as those of iEsop; in order to turn them from evil ways, they were frightened with terrible stories about Lamias, Gorgons, Ephialtes, Mormolyx, Empusa, and Manducus, the ogres and ogresses of antiquity. Then, as the empire of credulity is not limited to the days of childhood, people of all ages allowed themselves to be terrified by stories of evil spirits, spiteful genii by whom the air was peopled— phantoms and ghosts.

When, about the first century of the Christian era, the passion for magic took possession of the whole pagan world, this kind of marvellous story opened an unlimited field to the fancy of the narrator. We have already seen an indication of this in the *Heroica* of Philostratus. Love romances borrowed several of their episodes from fantastic stories; there is not a single one of them which dispenses with this method of affording pleasure, a sure means of gaining the approval of the readers of their time. How can we be astonished at this, when even history itself did not dispense with it, as we may see from the spirit which Plutarch introduces as appearing to Brutus before the battle of Philippi? The compilations of Apollonius and Phlegon of Tralles, which have been preserved to us under the title of "Wonderful Histories," contain several stories of this kind, with which, in some cases, is intermingled the artifice of an ingenious fiction. Lucian, in a dialogue called "The Liar," gives us a regular series of fantastic stories, which were current in his time, one of which has furnished Goethe with his story of the " Sorcerer Pupil." But, if the philosopher quizzed the superstitious beliefs of his time, the wit did not disdain to make use of them in his turn as the subject for his refined badinage. He is believed to be the author of *Lucius,* which he wrote by way of diversion, just as his contemporary, the Platonist Apuleius, amused himself with the *Metamorphoses.*

Was the work which we possess under the title of *Lucius* written by Lucian?1 Again, as there is no doubt that the subject produced at least two distinct works, one attributed to Lucius of Patras, and the other to Lucian, did the latter imitate the former? or has some forger imitated him while bringing his work out in the name of Lucius of Patras? These are questions which have exercised the minds of the critics. To us it seems clear that the subject was handled several times in Greek; it must be older than the version which has come down to us as the work of Lucian. One of the strangest scenes in the romance, the monstrous adventure of the ass with the lady of Patras, had its prototype in the stories of Pasiphae as told by the poets, and the daughter of Hippomenes as told by the historians. Photius, who had before him two Greek versions of this romance, one by Lucius, the other by Lucian, draws a comparison between 1 See *Introduction* to Lucian.

the two. He reproaches the pretended Lucius with having spoken of all these wonders and enchantments in the tone of a man who believes what he relates; he prefers the narrative of Lucian, which he considers a humorous attack upon pagan superstitions. Most assuredly the false Lucius did not believe in his own metamorphoses any more than the author of the Luciad; but there is this difference between the two works that, while the one related in a dull and uninteresting style anecdotes that were sufficiently insipid in themselves, the other gave charm to his extravagances by the liveliness of his narrative. It seems to us that those critics are wrong who refuse to admit Lucian as the author of this work; tradition has attributed it to him, and the style is not unworthy of him. What is there improbable in his having done for the stories of the marvellous what he has done in his *True History* for the stories of imaginary voyages?

One of the merits of *Lucius* is its brevity. On the other hand, diffuse prolixity is the chief fault of the Metamorphoses of Apuleius, a fault which is nowhere more appreciable than when dealing with humorous subjects. It is not known which of the two works has been imitated by Apuleius — that attributed to Lucius, or Lucian; but the author himself tells us that he is relating a *Greek* story. He further tells us that he has patched together various tales of the nature of the Milesian Fables. He thereby reveals to us the secret of his method of composition, which consists in repeating all the stories of the *Luciad,* and supplementing them by a number of accessory circumstances and episodical narratives. One only of these narratives is more valuable than the rest of the work—the story of *Psyche*. This is not original; it evidently comes from a Greek source, and goes back to a remote origin. This graceful story contrasts strangely with the licentious and sometimes obscene stories which Apuleius borrows from the *Luciad* or adds to it, with numerous immoral pictures which betray an age when the amours of Pasiphae and Leda were represented in the open amphitheatre.

Like the *Luciad* and the *Metamorphoses,* the work of Petronius owes its origin to the Milesian Tales, and contains others which, taken as a whole, are superior to those of the romance of Apuleius. Besides this, Petronius possesses the advantage of a purer style and a more probable story; but, as far as morality is concerned, the *Satyricon* is even more offensive in its outspokenness and more revolting in its cynicism than the *Luciad* and the *Metamorphoses*. In these works, vice is at least not flaunted complacently, and various immoralities (especially such as those of Encolpius and Giton) are at times vigorously lashed; whereas the *Satyricon* is a gallery of pictures which are worse than obscene. But, if we can man-

age to overcome the disgust with which such a picture inspires us, it is impossible to forget this description of the wandering and disorderly life led by some of the youths of Rome, those profligate scholars and professional poets, who delivered harangues upon virtue in houses of ill-fame, who plied the trade of parasites, and who were at once profligates and rascals. This work describes, in the liveliest colours, the vices which, in imperial Rome, had infected not only the citizens of the lower orders, but even members of the highest society. It is not surprising that it should have been confounded with the "history of the debaucheries of Nero, containing the details of all his immoralities, and the names of the profligate men and abandoned women who took part in them," a work written by Petronius a few hours before his death, and sent by his order to the Emperor.

The *Satyricon* supplements the *Satires* of Juvenal as a picture of Roman depravity, the extravagances of luxury, and the shocking inequality between the different classes. How vigorously the author sketches the stupidity and insolence of the wealthy! What a portrait is that of Trimalchion, the Amphitryon so arrogant towards his guests, the ignorant man so proud of his ignorance, the rich man who does not know the amount of his wealth, and who, hearing a "poor man" spoken of, asks what the term means; the master so merciless to his slaves, who has one of them flogged for dropping a silver dish, and afterwards orders the dish to be thrown upon the dung-heap, to show at one and the same time that he is an inexorably strict master and superior to all considerations of economy! If Roman literature had not supplied us with "The Banquet of Trimalchion," we should lack a characteristic feature of the picture of the Roman aristocracy, so senseless in its extravagances, whose most mad caprices were unable to exhaust their wealth. Cicero had shown its greed and brutality in the case of Verres; it was left for Petronius to show its absurdity in the case of Trimalchion. Nor is Trimalchion a fancy portrait; we can find traces of him here and there in the works of the period. The vast estates possessed by Trimalchion, to the number of which he is eager to add, so as to be able to go from Italy to Sicily over his own property, remind us of the immense estates *latifundia)* which, according to Pliny, were the ruin of Italy. And the melancholy reflections mingled with the descriptions of debauchery, the idea of death which is introduced after the most disgraceful witticisms, the banquet finished by the making of a will, strikingly remind us of the whim of a certain Pacuvius mentioned by Seneca, who wished that he could have the pleasure of being present at his own funeral. In decaying societies, there are never wanting protests against the corruption of manners and aspirations to a better state of things. But, of all those who express indignation at the boldness of vice, how many are there who are free from the disgraceful vices which they deplore? The virulent satires of Horace, Petronius and Juvenal do not prove that they had not themselves paid tribute to the vices of their times; their unblushing language scarcely tallies with virtue. The pure-minded are less inclined to lash vices, because this renders it necessary to describe them, than to praise the good and celebrate its triumphs. This was done in the second century by the Christian Dion Chrysostom. This honest man, the most philosophical of all the rhetoricians, and the greatest rhetorician of all the philosophers, filled in a manner amongst the heathen the office of a preacher of morality. We owe to him one of the few "moral tales" of antiquity, the *Huntsman,* or *Euboean History.*

This is not the only composition of Dion Chrysostom in which the purpose of amusing by means of an ingenious story and the idea of instructing by means of salutary moral lessons are found combined. In addition to his *Libyan Fable* and his dialogues intermingled with stories of Diogenes the Cynic, he had composed several pieces of the nature of panegyrics, in which narrative holds an important place, the details of which are so fictitious and the moral purpose so obvious, that we feel tempted to regard them as short moral stories. We are speaking of the *First Melancomas* and *Charidemus.* The *First Melancomas* commences with a story prepared with too obtrusive artifice. Dion meets a friend and speaks of an athlete who has recently been victorious; his interlocutor mentions another athlete, Melancomas, whom he opposes to the first as a model of beauty, manly vigour, and virtue; he praises this athlete highly, and leaves Dion delighted at what he has just heard. Melancomas is no doubt an imaginary personage, and Dion had been previously commissioned to sing his praises. But what a difference there is between the two works! The one has a purely authentic character, the other is purely imaginary. We should be glad to believe the same of the *Charidemus,* which also sings the praises of a virtuous athlete—praises also introduced by an ingenious story.

Whatever we may think of these compositions, there is no doubt that Dion's *Euboean History* is a moral tale, and a model of its kind. It precedes *Daphnis and Chloe,* and is certainly superior to the latter in truthfulness of description and purity of sentiment; it exhibits features worthy of the author of *Paul and Virginia.* It is a charming pastoral, the scene of which is well drawn, and the characters interesting, because they are real. Dion has enlivened his picture of rustic manners by describing two huntsmen instead of the shepherds, ox herds, and goatherds so familiar in eclogues. Their solitary but nevertheless happy life, poor yet hospitable, forms a striking but not too exaggerated contrast to the noisy, restless, and selfish life of the wealthy inhabitants of cities. Sons of outlaws, deprived of their inheritance, thrown from their earliest years upon the desert shores of Euboea, these two men have grown up, living on the produce of the chase and the lands which their own hands have cultivated; each has married his friend's sister and thus founded a family; their knowledge of other men is limited to the shipwrecked mariners whom they have assisted, and they would never have

known the city had not one of them been involuntarily led to it. While they were living thus, apart from the world, strangers to the burdens of society and the refinements of civilisation, without ever having reflected whether the land which they watered with the sweat of their brow legally belonged to them, an orator, eager to make a stir and greedy of popularity, denounced them as usurpers of the public domains, and one of them was dragged to the city to answer for himself before the magistrates. He was astounded at the sight of so many splendid houses, so many magnificent buildings, and the theatre filled by a crowd that was by turns noisy and silent; he appears without alarm before the multitude assembled to judge him for crimes which he does not even understand; he answers simply, and not without a shade of natural sarcasm, to the accusations of the demagogue whose aim is to destroy him; he repels with scorn the ridiculous charge of burying gold. One of those present, touched by his evident unhappiness, undertakes his defence, and soon striking evidence is given in favour of the poor huntsman; one of the citizens recognises in him his benefactor, the man who had formerly received him into his hut after a shipwreck. The story ends with a marriage; the author has supplemented his agreeable picture of pastoral life by a love episode, lightly handled, fresh and pure, which has nothing in common with the sensual pictures of *Daphnis and Chloe.* Perhaps Dion does not sufficiently conceal the moral idea which has inspired the story— the happiness of virtuous poverty. However, taken as a whole, the *Euboean History* shows us in Dion Chrysostom a worthy predecessor of Marmontel.

Lucius himself, the witty but licentious historian of the misfortunes of Lucius of Patras, has left us something that resembles the moral tale, in the dialogue called *Toxaris,* which is a collection of tales of Hellenic and Oriental colouring. The former are related by a certain Mnesippus, the latter by the Scythian Toxaris; the subject of both is, generous actions inspired by friendship. Lucian is careful to inform us that these stories are imaginary, but he does so in a roundabout and piquant manner. Mnesippus, the first narrator, swears by the gods that he will say nothing that is not true; this somewhat embarrasses Toxaris, who says: "I could have wished that you had not taken this oath, for I should have been able to dispense with believing you." Toxaris did not know the value of a Greek oath. However, being somewhat of a Greek himself, he repays his interlocutor in the same coin. Mnesippus also, less polished than the Scythian, says at the end of one of his stories, "That is really tragic. I should think it was a fable, if it were not for the respect due to the cemetery, and the wind by which you have sworn. I think that, without much offence to you, one might dispense with believing you."

It is curious to notice the important part played by the Oriental tale in the *Toxaris.* We have already seen in Herodotus, Ctesias, and Diodorus Siculus, more than one trace of it; but it is especially after the Roman period that the Oriental imagination is freely developed in Greek literature: in the *Life of Apollonius of Tyana,* in the *Lives of Pythagoras and Plotinus,* in the Romance of Antonius Diogenes, and in the apocryphal gospels; it is destined to flourish later in the more modern versions of the false Callisthenes, and in the *Life of Barlaam and Josaphat.* Lucian, through the mouth of his Scythian, takes the trouble to point out to us the difference between Greek and Oriental taste as exhibited in the *Toxaris.* "Do not expect," says Toxaris to Mnesippus, " incidents of friendship like those which you have recounted to me. What, in fact, did you say? That, out of devotion to a friend, one man married a very ugly girl without a dowry, that another gave two talents to bring about the marriage of a friend's daughter, that a third caused himself to be put in prison with the certainty of being set free a few moments afterwards. For my part, I shall relate to you the story of numerous massacres, of death faced on behalf of friends, and you will see that your exhibitions of friendship are mere child's play compared with those of the Scythians." Toxaris keeps his word, and his narratives reproduce faithfully the fondness of Orientals for exaggerated language, for extraordinary and marvellous facts. It is this character, combined with the sophistical genius of the Greeks, that is present in the majority of the romances of which we still have to speak, the authors of which all belong, by birth, to the East, by intellectual culture, to Greece.

One of the oldest of these works, in which the Oriental inspiration is most evident, is the romance of Iamblichus the Syrian. This author affords us the curious example of an Asiatic writing in Greek a story taken, as he himself tells us, from an Asiatic work. Photius, Suidas, and a marginal note in a manuscript of the *Bibliotheca* of Photius give us precise details in regard to this writer. He was a freedman, born at Babylon of Syrian parents. At first brought up in the language and manners of his countrymen, he was afterwards entrusted to the care of a Babylonian, who initiated him into the language, manners, and literature of Babylon. His master, who had been one of the king's secretaries, had been taken prisoner at the time of Trajan's entry into Babylon (a.d. 102) and sold to a Syrian. Later, Iamblichus learned the Greek language, which he spoke and wrote with ease and elegance, as is proved by his *Babylonica*. In this work he mentions the defeat of Vologeses by Verus, which took place about 162. He must, therefore, have been born and brought up between these two dates, 102 and 162, earlier rather than later. Photius speaks of the *Babylonica* in a complimentary manner which is not justified by his analysis: "Iamblichus is distinguished by beauty of style, the regularity and arrangement of his narrative. He should rather have employed all his efforts and all his art upon serious subjects, instead of wasting these qualities over puerile fictions. " In spite of the praises of Photius, the *Babylonica,* of all the romances up to the fifth century which have come down to us, is the one which contains the most improbable, the most confused, and the

most incoherent story. It is not, however, the least curious, for it is one of the oldest. We are surprised to find in it the germ of these erotic metaphysical discussions so much in fashion during the Middle Ages. A youthful coquette has given one of her lovers a cup, another her garland of flowers, a third a kiss. Which is the most favoured? The case is tried, and, after a debate, the decision of the judge, as may be imagined, is given in favour of the latter.

It is not easy to decide which romances belong to the Roman period, and which do not go beyond the Byzantine period. We have very few trustworthy details in regard to the authors; even their names seem to be, for the most part, fictitious. The date of their works can only be fixed by analogy and induction, which afford but slight evidence.

Two writers of the fifth century, Socrates and Sozomen, speak of *Heliodorus* and his *Theagenes and Chariclea.* The date of this work is thus assigned, by two authentic witnesses, to the fourth century. That is all we know for certain concerning this writer. The anecdote which shows us Heliodorus as obliged to choose between his bishopric and his romance, and renouncing the former, is only found in the monk Nicephorus Callistus, by no means a weighty authority. It is by no means proved that the author of the romance of *Theagenes and Chariclea,* who calls himself, at the end of his work, "a descendant of the race of the Sun," is identical with the Bishop of Tricca, who was famous for the severity with which he enforced ecclesiastical discipline. Socrates does not affirm the identity, but relates it as a simple tradition. What supports the tradition is, the high moral tone which distinguishes the romance, and the fact that a great deal of attention is devoted to Thessalian manners and customs; and Tricca was in Thessaly.

The romance of Heliodorus enjoyed, in its own time and during the whole Byzantine period, a great reputation, which it has never entirely lost. Three high authorities have recommended it: Amyot, who translated it; Racine, whose favourite reading it was in his youth; and Boileau, who draws a comparison between it and Fenelon's Telemachus. The first thing that strikes the reader is, that the romance is an olio; and from what works? The epic and tragic poems of antiquity. On every page we find imitations of Homer and Euripides, his chief models; by no means a merit, for a prose writer ought not to seek his inspiration amongst the poets. Heliodorus writes in prose, but he borrows the style, sometimes even the language of the poets; his romance is one of the earliest examples of *poetic-prose* works, which we cannot look upon favourably.

Theagenes and Chariclea is not only a romance in poetic prose; it is almost a prose epic poem, but a middle-class epic poem. Like the epic poets, and Herodotus their pupil, Heliodorus is careful to follow the order of the times; he flings us into the midst of the life of his characters; and it is only incidentally that he goes back to preceding events. His romance is conceived upon the plan of the Odyssey.

In like manner, the incidents are nearly all reminiscences of ancient Greek poetry. Heliodorus has not drawn largely on his own imagination; most of his episodes are taken from tragedies and epic poems. Although he has changed the names, multiplied details, and spread over his pictures his own effeminate and somewhat gloomy colouring, the episode of Cnemon and Demaeneta is the story of Phaedra and Hippolytus; Petosiris and Thyamis are the counterparts of Eteocles and Polynices; the incident of Hydaspis and Chariclea is the same as that of Agamemnon ready to sacrifice Iphigenia.

Not satisfied with borrowing from epic poetry, Heliodorus borrows from the marvellous. The Gods intervene in the affairs of Theagenes and Chariclea. If the author really believed in such intervention, we might tolerate the fables of Heliodorus; but this is not the case. Credulity and scepticism clash in this romance. We hear continually of oracles, dreams, apparitions, facts miraculously announced and accomplished; and, amidst all these marvels, we find a priest of Egypt, who, although interested in the general belief in these prodigies, himself shows us how he imposes on simple minds by such artifices. Calasiris affects to believe in such oracles, dreams, and revelations, and amuses himself by deceiving, with the aid of superstitious practices, the ingenuousness of Chariclea, Nausicles, and even his colleague, Charicles, the high priest of Delphi.

The purely human events described by Heliodorus are not much more probable — a defect common to all the Greek romances of that period. Anxious to excite surprise rather than interest, the writers endeavour to arouse curiosity by stories of singular events, at variance with real life; it seems as if improbability were one of the ruling principles of the Greek literature of the time. Desirous of striking the imagination of the readers, which was longing for something new, they abuse the picturesque, and scatter upon the path of their characters rocks, precipices, and, above all, caverns. There is not one of these romances in which there does not occur some adventure with brigands or pirates; but they are fancy brigands and pirates. The brigands of Heliodorus are the brigands of comic opera, who are quite capable of killing and robbing, but are not ignorant of the respect they owe to ladies. Chariclea twice finds herself in their power; she is at first a captive of Trachinus, who wishes to marry her, and gives her time to make up her mind; another time, she falls into the hands of Thyamis, who also wishes to marry her, but begins by calling his subjects, the pirates, to witness that he leaves her free to do as she pleases.

The greatest defect of the story is its somewhat excessive length. Heliodorus has merits; he has drawn his plot cleverly, and knows how to vary his episodes and connect them with the chief action; his style, in spite of its patchiness, is pleasant and graceful; but his work is one which we do not care to read again. He has not known how to create interesting situations or living characters.

We cannot deny the romance one merit—its moral tone. We are conscious

in it of the idea of the holiness of Christian marriage, which has inclined one of his editors to the belief that the author was at least a Christian. Certain moral developments are made the occasion of a homily; in general, however, the moral tone is more prominent in the narrative than in the reflections introduced. The author shows, with considerable art, the growth of faults from faults, and punishment brought about by the perversity of the guilty one. Thus, passion drives Demaeneta to the most cowardly vengeance, and Arsaces to the most atrocious cruelty, and remorse subsequently makes them both commit suicide. Taken altogether, the work of Heliodorus is the best of the Greek Romances later than the second century, with the exception of *Daphnis and Chloe.*

The merit of the latter does not consist in its moral tone. The story of *Daphnis and Chloe* is very simple, a quality which we appreciate, when we remember all the clumsily dramatic incidents which are heaped together in the other Greek Romances. Its style is anything but simple; the author was a man of elegant accomplishments, and possessed a fairly keen appreciation of nature,
but the work exhibits traces of decadence.
Nothing is known of the author, not even his name. How could a Greek writer bear the name of Longus? It has been conjectured, not without probability, that the Latin name is the result of an error in the reading of the MSS.
Suidas has a brief notice of Achilles Tatius, but it gives us few precise details. We merely learn from it that, after having composed the *Loves of Leucippe and Clitophon,* Achilles Tatius embraced Christianity and became a bishop.
His romance is not so well put together as *Theagenes and Chariclea.* It was an unfortunate idea to put the story into the mouth of the chief character, and to give him for his auditor an unknown person, who does not once interrupt the story, because it does not interest him.

The affected style, the hankering after antithesis, the numerous digressions, the prolix analysis of passions and emotions,
render it inferior to the romances of Longus and Heliodorus. Certainly, Tatius has the advantage of not being so diffuse as the latter; his faults are partly redeemed by the liveliness of the narrative,
and a certain vivacity apparently borrowed from the Greek comedians.
The romance of *Abrocome and Anthia,* by Xenophon of Ephesus, is certainly inferior to the works we have mentioned.
The story is unpleasant, and the incidents improbable. The style, however, is pure and natural, which has led to the belief that he was the earliest of the romance-writers. But this cannot be; the composition of the work is far too complicated for it to belong to a remote period, and the triviality of the style exhibits the decline of Greek literature. However, like *Leucippe and Clitophon* and *Daphnis and Chloe,* it can hardly be later than the fifth century of the Christian era. The colouring is too pagan for us to attribute these stories to a period when morals had been regenerated by Christianity. Filthy subjects, of which
Achilles Tatius and Xenophon of Ephesus speak with indifference, disappear from the Byzantine period; we find no trace of them in *Chacreas and Callirhoe,* by Chariton of Aphrodisias, in *Hysmine and Hysminias,* by Eumathius Macrembolites, or in the *History of Apollonius of Tyre,* who has the merit of describing an amour in which feeling plays a larger part than the senses. We do not mention the romances of Xenophon of Cyprus and Xenophon of Antioch, of which nothing but the names has come down to us, nor the verse romances of Theodorus Prodromus, Constantine Manasses, and Nicetas Eugenianus, which belong to the twelfth and thirteenth centuries.1

Hellodorus, bishop and famous Greek romance-writer, born at Emesa in Syria, lived towards the end of the fifth century of the Christian era, under Theodosius and his sons. He was descended from a family of priests of the Sun. In his youth, and perhaps before his conversion to Christianity, he composed a romance called *Aethiopica.* The time and cir 1 From *l'Histoire du Roman dans Vantiquité,* by A. Chassang. cumstances of his conversion are not known; but he is known to have become Bishop of Tricca in Thessaly. According to the ecclesiastical historian Socrates, he established the rule that every priest who did not separate from his wife after his ordination should be deprived of his office. Another ecclesiastical annalist, Nicephorus, relates that, on a provincial synod accusing the *Aethiopica* of being injurious to young people, the author was reduced to the alternative of agreeing to the suppression of his book or of losing his episcopal office. Heliodorus, if we may believe the historian, preferred to sacrifice his bishopric to his romance. Valois, Petau, Huet, and other critics have refuted this improbable story. Even if he had wished it, Heliodorus could not have suppressed his romance, and besides, nothing in the work called for measures so severe. The *Aethiopica* is irreproachable on the score of morality. As a literary production, it is the masterpiece of its kind amongst the Greeks.
The plot of Theagenes and Chariclea being somewhat intricately set forth, the following analysis, from *Dunlop's History of Fiction,1* may be of service:

"The action of the romance is supposed to take place previous to the age of Alexander the Great, while Egypt was tributary to the Persian monarchs. During that period a queen of Aethiopia, called Persina, having viewed at an amorous crisis a statue of Andromeda, gives birth to a daughter of fair complexion. Fearing that her husband might not think the cause proportioned to the effect, she commits the infant in charge to Sisimithres, an Aethiopian senator, and deposits in his hand a ring and some writings, explaining the circumstances of her birth. The child is named Chariclea, and remains for seven years with her reputed father. At the end of this period he becomes

such slaughter. Such was their opinion; but as yet they knew not the truth.

Meanwhile, the young girl hastened to the youth, flung her arms around him, wept and kissed him, wiped off the blood, uttered loud groans, and, although she held him in her grasp, seemed scarcely able to believe her eyes. When the Egyptians saw this, they altered their opinion. "How," said they, "can this be the act of a goddess? would she embrace a lifeless corpse so affectionately?" After this, they encouraged one another to take heart, and draw nearer and learn the truth. Their courage revived, they descended, and found the young girl still tending the other's wounds; standing behind, they remained motionless, venturing neither to speak nor to act. The girl, hearing the noise of their footsteps and seeing their shadows on the ground, looked up; in no way alarmed by their strange complexion, or their arms, which proclaimed them brigands, she lowered her eyes again, and devoted her whole attention to the prostrate youth. Thus the keenness of regret and the sincerity of love make us disregard all external objects whether pleasant or painful, and compel us to see nothing but the one beloved object, and to devote to it our whole attention.

III. When the brigands stopped in front of her, apparently intending to lay hands on her, she looked up again, and, seeing their dark complexions and hideous appearance, thus addressed them:

"If you are the shades of the dead that are lying here, you do wrong to trouble us; for most of you have died by your Meanwhile, another band of brigands came up, with two horsemen riding at their head. When the first band perceived them, without venturing to show fight or carry off any portion of the booty, for fear they might be pursued, they fled with all speed, being only ten in number, while those whom they saw coming were three times as many. Thus the young girl found herself captured a second time, although not actually a prisoner. The new arrivals, although intent on plunder, halted for a while, astounded at what they saw and ignorant of the cause. They imagined that those who had just fled had perpetrated the massacre, and seeing that the young girl, dressed in strange and magnificent attire, paid no attention to the dangers that threatened her, as if they had no existence, but devoted all her care to the young man's wounds, and seemed to feel his sufferings as if they were her own, they stood still, struck with admiration at her beauty and courageous spirit, while they were equally astonished at the form and stature of the own hands; those who were slain by us deserved their fate; we only exercised the right of self-defence to protect our honour. If you are living men, you would seem to be brigands; then you have arrived at a fitting moment to deliver us from our present calamities, and to end this scene of horror by our death."

Such was the tragic plaint she uttered. The others, unable to understand what she said, left the unhappy pair, thinking their weakness a sufficient guard; then, hurrying to the ship, they ransacked the cargo, which was considerable and consisted of various kinds of wares; to some they paid no heed, but carried off gold and silver, precious stones, and silken stuffs, as much as they could carry. When their greed was satisfied, they spread the booty on the shore, and divided it into equal portions, making the distribution not according to the value, but by the weight of each article. They had decided to defer the consideration of what they should do with their prisoners.

wounded young man, who had gradually recovered, while his features resumed their ordinary expression. IV. At length the captain of the band drew near, laid his hand upon the young girl, and commanded her to get up and follow him. Guessing what he meant (although she did not understand his words), she began to drag the young man along with her, who himself refused to part from her; then, pointing the dagger towards her breast, she threatened to kill herself, unless they took him as well. Her gestures, rather than her words, explained her meaning to the Captain, who, hoping that the young man, if he recovered, might be of great service to him, dismounted and ordered his esquire to do the same, and bade his prisoners mount in their places. Bidding his men collect the spoil and follow him, he himself walked on foot by the side of the captives, to hold them up in case they should be in danger of falling. Nor was their lot without its compensation; the master seemed to be the slave, and the captor the servant of the captured.

So true is it that the appearance of nobility and the sight of beauty is able to subjugate even the hearts of brigands and to conquer the harshest natures.

V. After the brigands had followed the coast for a distance of about two stades, they left the sea on their right, and turned aside in the direction of a mountain, which they climbed with difficulty, and, descending the other side with all speed, arrived at a lake which lay below. The whole district is called Bucolia (Pasture) by the Egyptians. In it there is a valley, which receives the overflow of the Nile and becomes a lake, very deep in the middle, while its shores are shallow and marshy; for the waters of lakes, like those of the sea, diminish in depth the nearer they are to the land. This spot is as it were the republic of all the brigands of Egypt. Some dwell in huts which they have built upon rising ground above the level of the water, while others live in boats, which they use both for habitation and purposes of transport; it is here that their wives spin, and are brought to bed. Their children are first brought up on their mothers' milk, afterwards upon fish caught in the lake and dried in the sun. As soon as a child can crawl, a cord is tied to its ankles, and it is allowed to go as far as the edge of the boat or the door of the hut, the cord being used as a guide.

VI. Thus those who are born on the lake look upon it as their nurse and native land, and regard it as a safe stronghold for brigands like themselves, who flock thither in large numbers. The water serves them as a wall, and the reeds, which grow in abundance, as a palisade. Amongst these reeds they have cut several winding and tortuous paths, easy

for themselves to find who know them, but which are difficult of access to others and form a strong defence against invasion. Such is this little republic, and such the manners of its inhabitants. VII. The sun was setting when the captain and his followers reached the lake. They made the prisoners dismount, and put the booty on board the boats. Those who had not taken part in the expedition issued in large numbers from different sidesof the marsh, and hurried to meet their chief, whom they received with as much reverence as if he had been a king. At the sight of the rich spoil and the divine beauty of the maiden, they imagined that some temple or shrine had been plundered by their companions, thinking, in their rustic simplicity, that they had carried off the priestess or the breathing image of some goddess. Then, with loud praises and congratulations, they escorted their chief in triumph to his abode.

This was a small island, apart from the rest, which he shared with a small number of intimate friends. As soon as he arrived there, he bade the multitude return home, after having ordered them all to assemble before him on the following day. He himself, with a few intimate friends, took a hasty supper, and then handed over the young couple to a young Greek, who had been taken prisoner by the brigands a short time before, that he might serve as interpreter; he lodged them in part of his own hut, and charged the Greek to pay careful attention to the young man, and, above all, to see that no insult was offered to the young lady. He himself, exhausted by the fatigues of his journey, and overwhelmed with the anxieties of command, soon fell asleep.

VIII. When silence reigned throughout the marsh, about the first watch of the night, the maiden took advantage of the solitude and the absence of those who were likely to disturb her, to give vent to her sorrow; the quiet of the night only increased her grief, since nothing was to be seen or heard that could divert her painful thoughts. Separated from the rest by the captain's order, and lying upon a miserable couch, she sighed and shed bitter tears: "O Apollo, how cruel is the punishment you inflict upon us, far greater than our offences deserve! Is not your vengeance satisfied with the misfortunes which we have already suffered? Deprived of our parents, captured by pirates, exposed to perils without number on the sea, a second time fallen into the hands of brigands—can worse than this await us? when will you put an end to our miseries? Provided I could die pure and without reproach, death would be welcome. But if anyone should dare to attempt to obtain by force the favours which even my Theagenes has never obtained, I would strangle myself and anticipate the insult; so would I keep myself pure and chaste, as I have hitherto done, even to the hour of death, and virtue itself should be my honourable shroud. No judge will ever be more pitiless than you, O Apollo!"

She would have proceeded, but Theagenes interrupted her: "Hush, my life, my dearest Chariclea! your laments are just, but they provoke the god more than you imagine. You must not reproach him, but invoke his aid. Prayers are more likely than accusations to appease the wrath of those who are mightier than ourselves." "You are right," she replied: "but, tell me, I beg you, how are you yourself?" "Better, since evening; this young man's attention has allayed the inflammation of my wounds." "You will find yourself much easier in the morning," rejoined their keeper: "I will apply a certain herb to your wounds, which in three days will heal them. I know its valuable properties by experience. Since I have been a prisoner here, when any of the Captain's followers return wounded from an expedition, I apply this remedy, which soon restores them to health. Do not be surprised if I sympathize with you; your lot seems to resemble mine; besides, since I myself am a Greek, I cannot help pitying you who are Greeks." "A Greek! Oh, heavens!" exclaimed the youthful pair, transported with joy. "Yes, most assuredly: a Greek both by birth and language." "Perhaps we shall obtain some alleviation of our sorrows. But by what name are we to call you?" "My name is Cnemon." "From what part of Greece do you come?" "From Athens." "What has been your history?" "Forbear," said Cnemon: "why do you attempt to revive the recollection of my sorrows? let us leave this to the tragedians; my story would be an unnecessary aggravation of your own misfortunes; besides, the rest of the night would not suffice to tell the tale, especially as you must need rest and sleep after all your fatigues." IX. But, as they persisted and begged Cnemon to tell his story, thinking that it would be a great consolation to them to hear of misfortunes equal to their own, he began as follows:

I am the son of Aristippus, an Athenian by birth, a man of considerable means, and a member of the Areopagus. After my mother's death, he married again; I was his only son, and he did not wish to be dependent upon my care alone in his old age. He married a lady, named Demaeneta, a most charming woman, but the cause of all my misfortunes. As soon as she entered the house, she endeavoured to make herself absolute mistress, and easily persuaded the old man to do whatever she wanted, by the charm of her beauty and the obsequious attention which she bestowed upon him; more than any woman I have ever known, she possessed the art of inspiring passion, and a wonderful knack of seducing those of the opposite sex. When my father went out, she wept; when he returned, she ran to meet him, complained of his long absence, and declared that, if he had delayed longer, it would have killed her; she embraced him after every word, and moistened her kisses with her tears. Ensnared by her artifices, my father saw no one but her, and lived for her alone.

At first she pretended to look upon me as her own son, thereby strengthening her hold upon my father. Sometimes she would kiss me, and desired that I would give her the pleasure of my company. I permitted her caresses, in no way suspecting the purpose she had in view; my only surprise was that she showed such motherly affection towards me. But when she grew more wanton, and her kisses became hotter

than decency permitted, and her looks immodest—all this aroused my suspicions, and I began to avoid and repel her advances. I omit the rest, why need I weary you with recalling it? the different ways in which she tempted me, the promises which she made; calling me her little boy, her darling, her heir, her life and soul, mingling with the tenderest names all that was most likely to win my affections; in more serious matters she played the part of a mother, but in dalliance clearly showed that she was in love.

X. At last, her passion declared itself. During the celebration of the great Panathenaic festival, the Athenians carry a ship through the streets in honour of Athena. I had just arrived at man's estate, and, after I had sung the usual hymn in honour of the goddess, and duly led the customary procession, I returned home, still wearing my ceremonial robes, my head still crowned with garlands. As soon as Demaeneta saw me, she lost her reason, and, no longer able to disguise her passion, ran towards me, calling me "her young Hippolytus, her darling Theseus." You can judge of my feelings at the time, seeing that the mere recollection of it makes me blush. That evening, my father supped in the Prytaneum; and, as was usual on the occasion of such meetings and public banquets, had arranged to pass the night there. During the night, Demaeneta entered my room, and endeavoured to obtain the satisfaction of her unholy desires. When I firmly resisted all her caresses, promises, and threats, she sighed deeply and left me; and, when only one night had passed, the accursed woman plotted revenge.

At first, she kept her bed in the morning, and, when my father returned, and asked her what was the matter with her, she pretended that she was indisposed, and at first refused to answer him further; but at last, yielding to his pressing enquiries, she said: "That wonderful young man, that son of yours, whom I looked upon as my own, whom (as the gods can testify) I loved even more than you did, observing, from certain indications, that I was with child, (which I had concealed from you until I was certain of it) took advantage of your absence, while I was admonishing him, as I have always done, and exhorting him to be temperate, and avoid women and drinking (for I was aware of his irregularities, but I would not disclose them to you, for fear you might suspect me as his stepmother)—while, I say, I was discussing these matters with him alone, to spare his blushes, he burst forth into such abuse of both of us, that I should be ashamed to repeat it; after which, he kicked me in the belly, and reduced me to the condition in which you now see me." XI. On hearing these words, my father, without saying anything to me, without questioning me or giving me time to defend myself, came to the conclusion that one who had shown such affection for me could not have accused me falsely. Chancing to meet me in the house, he attacked me with his fists, called his slaves and ordered them to scourge me, although I knew not for what I was being punished, a privilege usually granted to the greatest criminals. At length, when he had satisfied his anger, I said to him: "Now at least, my father, you ought to let me know for what crime I have been scourged, although you refused to tell me before." These words only provoked him more. "Deceitful wretch!" he cried, "is it from me that you would learn your infamies?" Then, turning away from me, he hastened to Demaeneta, whose rage, not yet satisfied, had laid a second plot to destroy me.

She had a maid called Thisbe, a handsome girl, who played admirably upon the lute. Demaeneta sent her to me with instructions to gain my affections. Without delay, she made advances to me; and she, who had oftentimes before rejected my suit, endeavoured to attract me by looks, signs, and gestures. In my vanity, I believed that I had suddenly become an Adonis, and at last, one night, I admitted her to my arms; she visited me a second and a third time, and indeed, on several occasions. But, when I exhorted her to take care that she was not surprised by her mistress, she said: "Oh, Cnemon, how simple you are! Do you think there is any danger for a slave such as I am, bought for a price, even if I am caught with you? if so, what punishment do you think my mistress deserves, a woman who boasts of noble birth, to whom the laws have assigned a husband, and who, although she well knows that death is the punishment of conjugal infidelity, is not afraid to commit adultery?" "Do not say so," I answered, "I cannot believe you." "Well, if you like, I will let you see her in the act." "If it is your wish," I said. "It is," she answered: "I desire for your sake, you have been so cruelly outraged by her, as well as for my own, who suffer terribly every day at her hands—the result of the bitter jealousy she feels against me. Therefore be a man, and surprise her with her paramour." XII. I promised, and she retired. Three nights afterwards, she came and woke me, telling me that Demaeneta was with her lover; that my father had been suddenly called into the country on business; and that the dishonourer of his bed had secretly, by appointment, entered his wife's room. She declared that it was my duty to prepare to avenge him and to arm myself with a sword, to prevent the villain's escape.

I did as she advised: I took a sword, and proceeded towards my father's room, while Thisbe carried a lighted torch in front. When I came to the door, I saw that there was a light burning inside; transported with rage, I broke upon the door, and rushed in, exclaiming, "Where is the wretch, the fine lover of this most virtuous woman?" With these words, I advanced, intending to run them both through with my sword. But, great heavens! my father leaped out of bed and fell on his knees before me, exclaiming: "Oh! my son, restrain yourself; pity your father; spare these grey hairs, that have brought you up. I have done you wrong, it is true; but death would be too cruel a vengeance. Do not abandon yourself to your rage, nor stain your hands with your father's blood."

Such were his piteous pleadings; for my part, as if smitten by a thunderbolt, I stood dumbfounded, unable to utter a word, looking for Thisbe, who had

stealthily withdrawn. I gazed at the bed and round the room, not knowing what to say or do. The sword fell from my hand; Demaeneta jumped out of bed, and seized it. When my father saw that he was out of danger, he laid hands upon me, and gave orders that I should be bound. Demaeneta, meanwhile, continued to exasperate him. "Did I not warn you of this?" she exclaimed; "did I not tell you to be on your guard against the youth, since he would seize the first opportunity of attacking you? I read his purpose in his eyes." "It is true," replied my father; "you warned me, but I refused to believe you." He then ordered me to be kept in chains, and refused to allow me to speak, or to tell him the real truth of the matter.

XIII. As soon as it was day, he took and led me, bound as I was, before the people; then, having poured ashes over his head, he thus addressed them: "Oh Athenians, it was not in expectation of this that I brought up my son; hoping that he would prove the support of my old age, I gave him, from his earliest years, a liberal education; after I had taught him the elements of letters, I introduced him amongst the members of his clan and family, registered his name amongst those who had reached the age of manhood, and secured him the standing of a citizen of our country, in conformity with the laws; in a word, my life's hopes were centred in him. But he, forgetting all this, first abused me and assaulted my lawful wife; and at last, with a naked sword in his hand, entered my chamber by night; if he is not guilty of the murder of his own father, he has only to thank Fortune, which inspired him with sudden terror, and caused the sword to fall from his hands. I now, therefore, have recourse to you, and formally denounce him. For although, according to the law, I might have slain him with my own hand, I did not wish to do so; I am content to leave the decision in your hands, for I am convinced that it is better that my son should be punished by the verdict of the law, rather than by death before a verdict has been pronounced." With these words, he began to shed tears.

Demaeneta also wept and pretended to be grieved at my sad lot. "Unhappy wretch!" she cried; "his death will be just, but premature; some avenging Deity has driven him to lift his hand against his parents." But her lamentations were not so much an indication of sorrow for me as a fresh evidence of the truth of the accusation.

In my turn, I asked permission to speak; but the clerk came forward and put the simple question to me: "Did you attack your father with a sword?" "I certainly did, but hear how that came to pass," I answered. Then all cried out that I had no right to ask to be heard in my defence. Some demanded that I should be stoned; others, that I should be handed over to the executioner; and others, that I should be thrust headlong into the Barathrum. As for myself, while all this disturbance was taking place and they were deciding what should be my punishment, I kept crying out: "Oh, stepmother! I am destroyed by a stepmother! a stepmother is taking away my life without a trial!" My words attracted the attention of some of the judges, and made them suspect the truth; yet even then they refused to listen to me; for the mind of the people was preoccupied by the incessant disturbance.

XIV. When the votes were counted, 1,700 were found to be in favour of putting me to death, some voting that I should be stoned; others, that I should be flung headlong into the Barathrum. The rest, to the number of 1,000—and that no doubt because their suspicions of my stepmother inclined them to mercy—were for condemning me to perpetual banishment. Their opinion gained the day; for, although the others, taken together, were in an actual majority, yet, as there had been a difference of opinion amongst them in regard to my punishment, the 1,000 votes formed a relative majority. Thus I was driven from my father's hearth and my native land. However, the gods did not suffer the wickedness of Demaeneta to go unpunished. I will tell you afterwards what happened to her. But now you must have some sleep; the night is far advanced and you need repose.

"By no means," said Theagenes; "you will only vex us still more, if you break off your story before telling us how this vilest of women was punished." "Listen, then," said Cnemon, "since such is your pleasure."

After the result of the trial I went down to the Piraeus, just as I was, and finding a ship there which was ready to set sail for Aegina, I embarked; for I remembered that some cousins of my mother lived there. On my arrival, I found those of whom I was in search, and at first I spent my time agreeably enough. About three weeks afterwards, in the course of my usual walk, I found myself down at the harbour; at the same moment, a bark was putting in to shore; and I waited a little to see where it hailed from, and who were on board. Almost before the ladder was properly let down, some one leaped on shore, hurried towards me, and embraced me. It turned out to be Charias, one of the friends of my youth. "I have good news for you, Cnemon," said he; "you are revenged upon your enemy. Demaeneta is dead." "Welcome, Charias," I said; "but why hurry over this good news so rapidly, as if you were the bearer of evil tidings? Let me have further details; for I am very much afraid that she has died a natural death, and has thus escaped the punishment she deserved." "Justice, to use the words of Hesiod, has not entirely deserted us; although she sometimes appears to wink at men's crimes, and to put off the day of punishment, nevertheless she casts her avenging eye upon such criminals; and it is she who has just punished the infamous Demaeneta. I know all that was said and done; you are aware of my relations with Thisbe; she told me everything. After the unjust sentence of banishment had been pronounced upon you, your unhappy father, regretting what he had done, retired into a lonely villa in the country, far from the haunts of men, and there he passed his days, 'eating his heart out,' in the words of the poet. As for Demaeneta, the Furies immediately began to torment her; your absence had only inflamed her passion for you; she never

ceased to weep, apparently for your misfortunes, but in reality for her own unhappy fate; night and day she cried, 'Oh, Cnemon, my dear, my darling boy, my well-beloved!' The ladies of her acquaintance, when they came to visit her, were astonished, and loudly praised her, because, although only a stepmother, she showed a mother's affection. They endeavoured to console her and restore her courage; but she answered that her sorrow was inconsolable, and that others did not know by what goads her heart was pierced.

XV. "Whenever she was alone, she bitterly reproached Thisbe for not having served her properly: ' How ready you were to do harm, how slow to assist me in my love! you hastened, almost before the words were uttered, to deprive me of all that I held most dear, Without even leaving me time to reflect or change my mind.' From these words, it was perfectly clear that she intended to do Thisbe a mischief.

"The latter, seeing how furiously indignant her mistress was, devoured by rage, and ready to plot against her, out of her mind, as she was, from anger and love, resolved to anticipate her, and, by laying a trap for her, to provide for her own safety. 'Why do you accuse your servant without cause, oh, my mistress?' said she; 'I have always, both now and in the past, studied your wishes; if anything has happened contrary to them, you must set it down to Fortune; I myself, even now, am ready, if you so desire it, to assist you in finding some remedy for your present distress. ' 'But what remedy can be found, my dear girl?' she asked; 'he who alone might have comforted me is far away, and the unexpected clemency of the judges has destroyed me. If he had been stoned, if he had been killed, my desire would have ended with his-life. For, when once all hope is lost, desire is extin guished in the soul; and the impossibility of reckoning upon anything in the future hardens the afflicted to sorrow. But now I seem to see him by my side, to hear his voice; he reproaches me with my unjust perfidy, and I blush for very shame to hear him. Sometimes I fancy that he will come back, and that I shall possess him; at other times I determine to go in search of him, wheresoever he may be. Such thoughts inflame my mind, they drive me mad. Oh Gods! I deserve my sufferings. Why, instead of trying to win his affection by kindness, did I plot against him? why, instead of supplicating him, did I pursue him with my hatred? He at first rejected my advances, as was only natural. I belonged to another, and, above all, he was ashamed to defile his father's bed. Perhaps time would have rendered him more tractable; persuasion might have induced him to yield. But I, cruel and savage beast that I was, treated him more like a tyrant than a mistress, and wrought a cruel deed against him, because he did not obey my commands and spurned the advances of Demaeneta, whom he far surpassed in beauty. But, my dear Thisbe, what is this easy remedy of which you speak?' 'Mistress,' she replied, 'it is generally believed that Cnemon left the city and Attica, in obedience to the sentence of banishment pronounced upon him; but I, who have made the most careful enquiries in your interest, have discovered that he is concealed somewhere in the neighbourhood of the city. You have no doubt heard of the flute-player Arsinoe; he was on intimate terms with her. After his misfortune, she received him, and, having promised to share his exile, is now hiding him in her house until she has made the necessary preparations for the journey.' 'Happy Arsinoe,' cried Demaeneta; 'how I envy your former relations with him, and the exile into which you are now going to accompany him! But, what has all this to do with us?' 'Much, my mistress,' replied Thisbe; 'I will pretend that I am in love with Cnemon, and I will ask Arsinoe, with whom I have long had professionalrelations, to introduce me to him some night in her stead. If she consents, it will rest with you to represent that you are Arsinoe and to take her place by his side. I myself will take care that he does not go to bed until he has drunk pretty freely. If you obtain what you desire, in all probability your passion will be cured; for very frequently the first experience extinguishes the flame of desire; when we have once got what we want, love is sated. If, however, your passion continues (which heaven forfend!), we must set sail again, in the words of the proverb, and try some other scheme. Meanwhile, let us think about the present.' XVI. "Demaeneta eagerly embraced the proposal, and begged Thisbe to put it into execution without delay. Having asked her mistress to allow her a day to make all necessary arrangements, she hurried to Arsinoe, and asked her if she knew Teledemus. When Arsinoe answered that she did, Thisbe said, 'Will you let us come to your house this evening, for I have promised to see him to-night? He will come first, and I will follow, after I have put my mistress to bed.' Thisbe then hurried into the country to Aristippus, and said to him: 'Master I am come to accuse myself before you; punish me as you think fit; I helped to ruin your son, against my will indeed, but nevertheless I did so. Knowing that my mistress led a dissipated life and defiled your bed, I feared some misfortune for myself, in case anyone discovered what was going on; but, above all, I was grieved to see you so ill-rewarded for the affection which you bestowed upon your wife. Being afraid, however, of revealing the state of affairs to you, I told my young master; I went to him by night, that no one might know anything about it, and told him that my mistress was in the habit of sleeping with a lover. He, being (as you know) already embittered against her, thought that I meant that a lover was actually in her room, and, in a transport of ungovernable rage, he seized a sword, and ran madly towards your chamber. I did my utmost to hold him back, assuring him that there was no one in the room at that moment; he paid no heed to what I said, or perhaps he thought that I had repented and changed my mind. The rest you know. Now, if you wish, you can at least clear your son's character, although he is now in exile, and punish her who has done you so much injury. This very day I will show you Demaeneta in bed with her lover, and, what is worse, in a strange

house, outside the city.' 'If you show me this,' said Aristippus, 'your freedom shall be your reward. Life will always be unendurable, until I have punished this enemy of my household. For a long time I have been tortured by anxiety; but, although I suspected her, I remained silent, for want of convincing proofs. But what must I do now?' 'You know the garden in which the Epicurean monument stands; go and wait for me there in the evening.' XVII. "With these words, she returned to the house, and went to find Demaeneta. 'Come,' she said, 'dress yourself carefully; you must keep the appointment in an elegant attire. I have arranged everything as I promised you.' Demaeneta dressed herself according to Thisbe's instructions. When evening came, Thisbe took her to the place of assignation. When they were close to the house, she bade her wait a little; then she went on and asked Arsinoe to go into another room and leave her undisturbed, being desirous, as she said, of sparing the young man's blushes, since he had only recently been initiated into the mysteries of love. Having without difficulty persuaded Arsinoe, she went out, and fetched Demaeneta, took her into the house and put her to bed. Then she took away the light, in order, as she pretended, that she might not be recognised by you, (who were at the time in Aegina), and bade her satisfy her passion without saying anything. 'I myself,' she said, 'will now go and find the young man and bring him to you. He is drinking somewhere in the neighbourhood.' As soon as she was outside, she ran to find Aristippus at the place which had been agreed upon, and urged him to go without delay, and bind the adulterer fast. He followed her, and, when he arrived at the house, rushed into the room, found his way to the bed as well as he could by the dim light of the moon, and exclaimed, 'Now I have caught you, oh! accursed woman.' While he was speaking, Thisbe rattled the doors as loudly as she could, and cried out, 'What untoward misfortune! her paramour has escaped. Mind you do not fail a second time.' 'Make yourself easy,' he answered, 'I have the abandoned woman in my power; it was she whom I wanted most.' With these words he seized her and dragged her towards the city. Demaeneta, reflecting, no doubt, upon her terrible situation, the disappointment of her hopes, her present disgrace, and the punishment which awaited her at the hands of the law, enraged at having been surprised, and furious at having been deceived, seized the moment when she was passing by the pit which is in the Academy (you know the place where the generals offer sacrifice to the shades of the heroes), suddenly tore herself from the hands of the old man, and leaped headlong into the pit. Thus the miserable woman perished by a miserable death.

"Thereupon Aristippus exclaimed, 'I have obtained satisfaction from you, without having recourse to the law.' On the following day, he laid everything before the people, and having with difficulty obtained pardon, went round amongst his friends and acquaintances, to consult them as to the best means of securing your return. I cannot tell you whether anything has been done; for, as you see, being summoned here on private business, I set sail before anything had been decided. You may, however, feel sure that the people will agree to your return and that your father will come and fetch you; he has announced his intention of doing so." XVIII. This was what Charias had to tell me. As for the rest of my story, how I came here, what I have gone through, it would take up too much time to tell.

With these words, he shed tears; the strangers did the same, apparently moved by the tale of his misfortunes, but really at the memory of their own. Their lamentations would never have ceased, had not sleep, induced by the luxury of their grief, suddenly come upon them and dried their tears. Thus, then, they went to sleep. In the meantime, Thyamis (this was the robber chieftain's name), who had rested quietly during the greater part of the night, was afterwards tormented by wandering visions; and, pondering what could be the meaning of the dream, he lay awake all night, plunged in meditation. It was the hour when the cocks begin to crow, either because a natural instinct warns them of the return of the sun to earth and they are moved to salute the god, or because a feeling of warmth and an eager desire to move and eat inclines them to rouse to work those who live in the same house. At this moment the gods sent Thyamis a vision.

He thought that he was in Memphis, his native country; he entered the temple of Isis, which seemed to be one blaze of lamps; the altars were full of all kinds of victims, and dripping with blood; the vestibule of the temple and its open spaces were filled by a noisy and agitated crowd. After he had entered the sanctuary, the goddess came forward to meet him, and presenting Chariclea to him, said: "Thyamis, I intrust this maiden to your care; you shall possess her without possessing her; you shall be guilty of a crime, you shall cover the stranger with blood, but she shall not die." This vision sorely troubled him: after turning the words over every way in his mind, in order to discover their meaning, he at last gave up the attempt, and interpreted them in accordance with his own desires. "You shall possess her without possessing her," he interpreted to mean that he should have her as a wife, not as a virgin; by the words "you shall cover her with blood," he understood the wounds inflicted upon her virginity, wounds which would not prove mortal. In this manner he explained the vision, agreeably to the suggestions of his passion.

XIX. As soon as it was day, he summoned his chief followers, and ordered them to bring the plunder, which he called by the high-sounding name of "spoils," into the midst; he also sent for Cnemon, with instructions to fetch the prisoners who had been intrusted to his care. While they were being conducted to the chief, they exclaimed, "What fate is reserved for us?" and begged Cnemon to assist them in any way he could. He promised to do so, and bade them be of good cheer, assuring them that the chief of the brigands was not an utter barbarian, but was of a kind and gentle disposition; that he belonged to an illustrious

family, and had only adopted his present mode of life from necessity.

When they reached his presence, and the whole band had assembled, Thyamis took his seat upon an eminence in the island, the appointed meeting-place, and ordered Cnemon to translate what he said to the prisoners; for, while he had only an imperfect knowledge of Greek, Cnemon had now learned to speak Egyptian. Thyamis then addressed the meeting as follows: "Comrades, you know what my feelings towards you have always been. You are aware that, being the son of a priest of Memphis, deprived of my right of succession to the sacerdotal functions, of which a younger brother, after my father's death, had robbed me, in violation of the laws, I took refuge amongst you, in order to avenge myself and recover my dignity. You thought me worthy to be your leader; since then, I have lived with you, without ever claiming any special privileges for myself. When there was money to be distributed, I was content with the same share as each of yourselves; when prisoners were sold, I paid what they fetched into the common stock; for I considered it the duty of a good leader to take upon himself the greatest share of fatigue and to be content with an equal share of the spoils. As to the prisoners, I have enrolled amongst your band those who, from their bodily strength, were likely to be useful to us, and sold the weaker. I have never been guilty of violence towards the women; those of noble birth I have released either on payment of ransom, or out of pure compassion for their lot; those of lower rank, who were condemned to slavery by habit rather than the rights of war, I have distributed amongst you as servants. On the present occasion, I ask nothing from you out of all this booty, except this stranger maiden; although I might have claimed her by right, I yet think it better to receive her from you by common consent; for it would be foolish to seem to be acting against the wishes of my friends by appropriating a prisoner by force. However, I do not ask even her from you for nothing; in return, I resign all share in the rest of the booty. The priestly caste despises indiscriminate love; I have made up my mind to wed this maiden, not to satisfy my lust, but in order to propagate my family.

XX. "I will also tell you the reasons which have led me to act thus. In the first place, she appears to me to be well n; this I conjecture from the money nd upon her, and also because she is by means overwhelmed by her misfortunes, t from the first has met them boldly. iNext, I am convinced that she is of a good and virtuous disposition; for if, while she surpasses all in beauty, she yet imposes respect upon all who see her by her modest looks, how can we help thinking highly of her? An even still more weighty reason is, that she seems to me to be the priestess of some god, since, even in her misfortune, she considers it an offence against religion to put off her garlands and sacred vestments. XXI. "Could any union be more fitting than that of a priest and priestess?" All applauded his words, and wished him a happy marriage, under favourable auspices. Then Thyamis continued: "I thank you, my friends; but we shall now do well to enquire what the maiden thinks about the matter. If I were disposed to make use of the right of authority, my wish alone would be sufficient; for those who can command obedience have no need to ask. But, in the case of lawful marriage, mutual consent is necessary." Then, addressing himself to Chariclea, he said: "What do you think of the proposal that we should marry? Tell me, who you two are, and who are your parents?" Chariclea remained for a long time with her eyes fixed upon the ground, shaking her head from time to time, as if she were collecting her thoughts before answering. When at length she lifted her eyes towards Thyamis, her beauty dazzled him even more than before; for her cheeks, animated by her thoughts, were ruddier than usual, and her kindling eyes were full of vehemence. Then, Cnemon acting as interpreter, she thus addressed Thyamis: "It would be more seemly that my brother Theagenes should answer; for I think that silence becomes a woman, and that it is a man's duty to answer amongst men. XXII. "But, since you have invited me to speak, and have given us in this the first proof of your humanity, showing that you wish to obtain what you have a right to claim by persuasion rather than by force (since everything that has been said concerns myself), I feel compelled to abandon my usual practice and that of my sex, and, even in the presence of so large an audience of men, to reply to the question put to me by him who is now my master. Listen, then, to the following account of us:

"We are Ionians: our family is one of the most illustrious in Ephesus. When we had attained to years of discretion, we were summoned by the law to undertake priestly functions; I was consecrated to Artemis, and my brother to Apollo. These functions last a year. When our term was over, we had to set out for Delos on the sacred embassy, to arrange the athletic sports and contests of music, and to lay down our priestly office in accordance with the established custom. For this purpose, a vessel was loaded with gold, silver, garments, and all that was necessary to invest with suitable dignity the public feast and entertainments. We set sail; our parents, already advanced in years, being afraid of the sea and the voyage, remained at home; but a large number of the citizens accompanied us, either on board our vessel, or upon others which they had fitted out themselves. When the voyage was nearly over, a storm suddenly arose; a violent hurricane, accompanied by thunder and lightning, lifted up the waves, and drove the ship out of its course; the pilot, obliged to yield to the fury of the storm, abandoned the helm, and allowed the vessel to drift haphazard. Seven days and seven nights we were borne along by the wind that never ceased, until at last we were cast upon the shore where we were found by you, and where you saw the traces of the great slaughter that had taken place. I must explain how it happened. The sailors conspired against us, while we were celebrating a feast in thanksgiving for our preservation, and resolved to kill

us and seize our property. A terrible struggle ensued, in which all our companions perished, while the sailors themselves slew and were slain: we alone survived the disaster—and would to Heaven we had not!—we alone remain, a miserable remnant. Our only consolation amidst our misfortunes is, that some god has brought us into your hands; and that we, who feared for our lives, have been granted permission to discuss the question of my marriage, which I certainly do not desire to decline. The idea that I, a captive, should be considered worthy of my master's bed, is indeed too great a happiness! and further, that a maiden, consecrated to the service of God, should be united to the son of a priest, who will soon, with Heaven's approval, be a priest himself, this is clearly the work of divine Providence. I only ask you, Thyamis, to grant me one favour: let me first go to the city, or wherever there is a temple or altar dedicated to Apollo, to lay aside my priesthood and deposit there these badges of my office. The best thing would be to wait until you return to Memphis, when you receive the dignity of priesthood; in this manner, our marriage would be more joyful as being associated with victory and celebrated after success. However, I leave it to you to decide whether it shall take place sooner; let me only first perform the sacred rites enjoined by the custom of my country. I know that you will grant my request, since, as you say, you have been devoted to the service of the gods from your infancy, and you are full of respect for everything that concerns them." XXIII. With these words she left off speaking, and began to weep.

All those who were present approved, and urged her to do as she proposed, and declared that they were ready to support her. Thyamis also approved, willing and yet unwilling. His passion for Chariclea caused him to look upon the delay of a single hour as an eternity. But, on the other hand, her words, like some siren's song, charmed him and compelled him to assent. Besides, he saw in this some connection with his dream, and believed that the wedding would be celebrated at Memphis. Having distributed the booty, he dismissed the assembly; he himself obtained some of the most valuable articles, a voluntary gift from his comrades.
XXIV. They were ordered to hold themselves in readiness to proceed to Memphis in ten days' time. He assigned the same tent to the young Greeks as before, and ordered that Cnemon should attend them, no longer as their custodian, but as their friend and companion. He also gave them more luxurious food than he ate himself, and sometimes invited Theagenes to his table, out of regard for his sister. He had resolved to see Chariclea only rarely and at intervals, for fear the sight of her might still more inflame his violent passion and drive him to do something contrary to the agreement that had been entered into. For these reasons Thyamis avoided her presence, thinking that, if he saw her, he would find it impossible to restrain himself.

As soon as the meeting had broken up, and all had dispersed to their several quarters in the marsh, Cnemon went some little distance from the lake, to look for the herb which he had promised Theagenes the day before.

XXV. Meanwhile Theagenes, taking advantage of the freedom afforded him, began to weep and sob; he did not address a word to Chariclea, but called upon the gods without ceasing. Thereupon the maiden asked him whether he was only lamenting their common misfortunes, or whether anything fresh had happened. "What fresh misfortune could be worse?" replied Theagenes; "what greater infidelity, what greater violation of vows and promises could there be than that Chariclea should forget me, and consent to another union?" "Hush!" said the maiden; "be not more cruel to me than my misfortunes; do not, after so many proofs of my fidelity in the past, suspect me in consequence of words uttered under stress of circumstances, and adapted to the necessities of the moment. Otherwise, you will show that you are changed yourself rather than that you have found any change in me. I am ready to endure unhappiness; but no force in the world will ever persuade me to do anything that virtue forbids. I know that in one thing alone I am immoderate—my passion for you; but this is lawful and honourable. I did not yield to you as a lover; I abandoned myself entirely to you from the first, as a husband with whom I had made a solemn compact; hitherto, I have kept myself pure from all illegitimate intercourse with you; I have frequently repelled your advances, waiting for the opportunity of legitimately consecrating that union to which we have been pledged from the commencement, and which has been confirmed by most solemn oaths. Besides, you could not be so foolish as to think that I should prefer a barbarian to a Greek, a brigand to one whom I love!"

"What, then, was the meaning of your fine speech?" asked Theagenes; "your idea of calling me your brother was a very wise precaution, which prevented Thyamis from being jealous of our affection for each other, and allowed us to associate freely and without fear. I understood that all you said about Ionia and our wanderings in the neighbourhood of Delos were so many fictions to disguise the truth and to mislead your hearers.

XXVI. "But, when you showed yourself so ready to agree to the proposal of Thyamis, definitely promised to marry him, and even fixed the day, I neither could nor would understand what it meant; rather, I wished that the earth had opened and swallowed me up before I had lived to see such a result of my hopes and labours on your behalf. " At these words Chariclea embraced Theagenes, covered him with kisses, and watered his face with her tears. "How delightful to me are your fears on my account! They prove that your love for me is not shaken, in spite of our calamities. Be assured, Theagenes, that had I not made this promise, we should not be conversing together at the present moment. Resistance, as you are aware, only aggravates a violent passion; whereas yielding words, calculated to humour the will, soothe its first outbursts, and blunt the edge of desire by the delights of which they hold out

promise in the future. Those who love most fiercely consider a first attempt implies consent, and, thinking that possession will follow, grow calmer, resting on their hopes. This consideration made me yield to Thyamis in words, leaving the future issue to the gods and the Genius who, from the beginning, has taken our love under his protection. An interval of a day or two is often most salutary, and Fortune brings means of safety which no human wisdom can devise. Wherefore I have deferred the present by my inventiveness, putting off the certainties of the present by the uncertainties of the future. Wherefore, my dearest, we must use this fiction as a wrestler's trick and conceal it not only from the rest, but even from Cnemon. For, although he is kindly disposed to us, and is a Greek, he is, like ourselves, a prisoner, and therefore more likely to try and gain his master's favour, should the opportunity occur. Neither the time our acquaintance has lasted nor the ties of kindred race are sufficiently sure pledges of his fidelity to us; wherefore, should he at any time touch upon the truth, you must flatly deny it. For a lie is sometimes permissible, even praiseworthy, when it benefits those who tell it and does no harm to those who hear it. " XXVII. While Chariclea was thus suggesting to Theagenes the best course to take, Cnemon entered in great haste, with agitation depicted in his looks. "Oh, Theagenes!" said he, "here is the herb which I promised you; take and apply it to your wounds. But we must be prepared for other wounds, and another massacre such as that you have already witnessed." Theagenes begged him to explain himself more clearly. "It is not the time to tell you now," he answered; "there is reason to fear that words might be anticipated by deeds. But follow me without delay, both you and Chariclea. " He then conducted them both to Thyamis, whom they found polishing his helmet and sharpening his spear, and said to him: "Your employment is opportune; gird on your arms and order your comrades to do the like. We are threatened by foes more numerous than we have yet encountered; they are close upon us; I descried them advancing over the top of the hill, and have hastened with all speed to announce their approach. I have also warned all those whom I met to get ready for battle." XXVIII. At these words, Thyamis started up, and asked where Chariclea was, as if he feared more for her than for himself. When Cnemon showed her trembling at the entrance of the tent, Thyamis whispered in his ear: "Take her into the cave where all our treasures are stored; and when you have taken her down, close the entrance in the usual way, and come back to me with all speed; we must make arrangements for the fight." At the same time he ordered his armourbearer to bring him a victim, that he might offer sacrifice to the gods of the place, before beginning battle.

Obedient to orders, Cnemon led away Chariclea, who sighed and lamented and kept looking back at Theagenes, and shut her down in the cave. This cave was not the work of nature, like many others that are hollowed out on the surface and in the interior of the earth. The art of the brigands had imitated nature, and had cleverly hollowed it out as a receptacle for their spoils.

XXIX. It was constructed in the following manner: Its entrance was narrow and dark, made beneath the door of a secret chamber, the threshold of which was another door, which easily shut and opened upon the entrance, and afforded a passage for descent, whenever necessary; within were a number of winding paths, cut at haphazard. These paths or galleries, sometimes separate and winding alone, sometimes purposely connected and intertwined like roots of trees, all converged into an open space at the bottom, which was dimly lighted through an opening in the lower part of the marsh. Here Cnemon made Chariclea descend; he led her by the hand to the inmost recesses of the cave, along the winding passages with which he was familiar, encouraging her in every way he could, and promising to return for her in the evening with Theagenes, whom he said he would not permit to take part in the coming engagement, but would keep him out of the way. Chariclea did not utter a word; she appeared stricken to death, deprived of Theagenes, her life and soul. He left her scarcely breathing and silent, and came up from the cave. Then he shut down the door, shedding tears over her lot and the necessity which compelled him to bury her alive, and to deliver over to darkness and obscurity the most beautiful of human beings. After this, he hastened back to Thyamis, whom he found burning with eagerness for the fray, and splendidly armed, with Theagenes by his side. In order to arouse to frenzy the warlike spirit of his comrades who surrounded him, he stood up in the midst, and thus addressed them:

"Comrades, I know that I need not exhort you at length; you want no encouragement, for you have always looked upon war as the breath of life. Besides, the sudden approach of the enemy cuts short all lengthy discourse. Those who, when the enemy attacks them, do not promptly prepare to repulse them by the same means, show themselves utterly ignorant of their duty. Know, then, that it is not a question of defending your wives and children, which alone in the case of many would be sufficient to rouse their spirits to battle; for these and other like advantages to which we attach less importance, together with those that victory brings, will remain ours if we overcome our foes. But it is a question of our very existence, of our life; no quarter is given, a truce is unknown in wars between pirates; life is the reward of victory, defeat is death. Let us therefore fall upon our hated foes with fury of mind and body." XXX. Having said this, he looked round for his squire, Thermuthis, and called him several times by name. When he did not appear, he burst out into violent threats against him, and hastened to the ferry. For the battle had already begun, and he was able to see from a distance the inhabitants of the extremity and approaches of the marsh in the hands of the enemy, who had set fire to the boats and huts of those who had fallen or sought safety in flight. The flames spread to the neighbouring morass, and consumed the reeds which grew there in

great abundance; the conflagration shed around a mighty and intolerable blaze, that dazzled the eyes, while the ears were stunned with the sharp crackling and roaring of the flames.

War, in every form and shape, was seen and heard; the inhabitants sustained the combat with all possible courage and vigour; but the enemy, who possessed the advantage of superior numbers and the suddenness of their attack, slaughtered some upon land, and overwhelmed others in the marsh with their boats and huts. In the midst of the tumult, a dull and confused sound rose in the air, as if the engagement were going on both on land and water; the combatants slew and were slain; the waters of the lake were stained with blood, and all were confusedly mingled with fire and water. Thyamis, at this sight and the terrible noise, suddenly remembered the vision, in which he had seen Isis and her temple, resplendent with lamps and full of victims for sacrifice; he saw in it the representation of what he now beheld, and, putting quite a different interpretation upon it from his earlier one, he thought that the words "you shall possess her, and yet shall not possess her," signified that Chariclea would be carried off from him by war, and that the words "you shall slay her and not merely wound her" referred to the sword, and not to the contest of love. He heaped abuse upon the goddess for having deceived him; and, exasperated at the thought that another should possess Chariclea, he bade his comrades halt, and, if they were obliged to fight, to carry on a war of ambuscade where they stood, and make secret sallies into the marshes around them, although even thus they would find it difficult to resist the enemy's superior numbers.

He himself, under pretence of going to look for Thermuthis, and offering up prayers to his household gods, gave orders that no one should follow him, and returned, almost beside himself, to his tent. It is in the nature of barbarians not to allow themselves to be turned aside from the object they have in view; when they despair of their own safety, they begin by slaying all those whom they hold most dear, either in the false belief that they will be with them again after death, or that, in so doing, they are delivering them from the violence and insults of the enemy. Thus Thyamis, forgetting all the dangers by which he was threatened, at the very moment when the enemy surrounded him like a net, raging with anger, love, and jealousy, hurried with all speed to the cave, and leaped down, crying out with all his might in the Egyptian language. At the entrance he found a woman who addressed him in Greek; her voice guided him to her person; he seized her hair with his left hand, and plunged his sword into her bosom.

XXXI. The unhappy woman uttered a piteous groan, and fell lifeless on the ground. Thyamis hastened up, closed the entrance, and flung a few handfuls of earth upon it, saying: "Let this be my wedding present!" He then made his way to the boats, where he found his companions preparing to take to flight, since the enemy could be seen close at hand; at the same time, Thermuthis arrived with a victim for the sacrifice. Thyamis reviled him, told him that he had anticipated him by offering the most beautiful of victims, and got into a boat, accompanied by Thermuthis and a rower, these boats, consisting of a single piece of wood and rudely hollowed out of the trunk of a tree, being unable to hold more than three. Accordingly, Theagenes and Cnemon got into another boat, and the rest did the same. When all had embarked, they retired to a little distance from the island, and at first rowed round it instead of going out into the open sea; soon they even ceased rowing, and drew up their boats in line, ready to meet the attack of the enemy. But, at the mere approach of the latter, as soon as they saw them, the brigands took to flight, frightened at the violence of the waves alone1 and thrown into confusion by the sound of their war cry. Cnemon and Theagenes also retreated, but not from fear. Thyamis alone, either because he thought it would be disgraceful to flee, or because he could not endure the idea of surviving Chariclea, rushed into the midst of his enemies.

XXXII. Already he was engaged with them, when some one cried out, "It is Thyamis; do not lose sight of him." Then immediately the boats surrounded and shut him in on all sides. He fought stoutly, wounding some and killing others; but the most astonishing thing was what happened afterwards; in spite of their numbers, not one of the enemy lifted up the sword, or hurled a javelin against him; their only object seemed to be to capture him alive. For a long time Thyamis resisted with all his might; but at last, a body of men rushed upon him, and tore his spear from his hands. He also lost his armour-bearer, who had bravely assisted him, but at length, believing 1 The word *podiov* might also mean "the shouts (of the enemy)." himself mortally wounded, and despairing of his life, flung himself into the lake, swam out of reach, and, although with considerable difficulty, safely gained the land, since the enemy did not think it worth while to pursue him; for, as they had already captured Thyamis, they regarded this as a complete victory. The loss of a great number of their comrades grieved them less than the capture alive of the man who had been chiefly responsible for it. So true is it that all brigands hold money dearer than life itself, and the rights of friendship and kinship are sacrificed to greed alone. It was so in this case; for the victors were the very same who had formerly taken to flight before Thyamis and his comrades at the Heracleotic mouth of the Nile.

XXXIII. Indignant at being deprived of that which was not really theirs, and as furious at the loss of the spoils as if they had been their own property, they gathered together their comrades who had remained at home and called upon the neighbouring villages for assistance, and, offering theman equal share of any spoils that might be taken, put themselves at the head of the expedition. The following was the reason why they took Thyamis alive. He had a brother named Petosiris living at Memphis, who had by intrigue dispossessed him of the dignity of chief priest, contrary to the custom of the country (for he was the younger brother). This Petosiris, having heard

that his elder brother had become the captain of a band of brigands, and being afraid that, if he found an opportunity, he might return to Memphis, or that time might reveal his treachery; and, in addition, seeing that he was suspected of having made away with his brother, who had disappeared, he sent messengers into the villages inhabited by the brigands, offering a large sum of money and a large number of cattle to any who should capture Thyamis alive and bring him to him. The brigands, seduced by these offers, even in the heat of battle did not forget the hope of gain held out to them; and, as soon as Thyamis was recognised, did not hesitate to sacrifice a number of their comrades, BOOK II in order to take him alive. When they had captured him, they put him in irons and rowed him to land, half of their number being deputed to guard him, while he reproached them bitterly for their apparent humanity and expressed greater indignation at his imprisonment than if it had been death itself. The others, meanwhile, returned to the island, in the hope of finding the treasures and booty of which they were in search, and scoured it thoroughly, leaving no part unexplored. But, finding nothing of all that they had set their hearts upon, with the exception of a few articles of trifling value, which the owners had forgotten to hide in the underground cave, they set fire to the tents. Then, since night was approaching, being afraid to remain longer in the island, lest they should fall into the hands of those who had escaped from the battle, they returned to their comrades. END OF BOOK 1

I. Thus the island was ravaged by fire; but Theagenes and Cnemon did not perceive the mischief as long as the sun was above the earth. For the appearance of fire is effaced by day, being illumined by the beams of the god. But, when the sun set and brought back the night, the flames, recovering their irresistible brilliancy, were clearly seen from afar. At the same time, Theagenes and Cnemon, trusting to the darkness of night, left the marsh, and beheld the whole island in a blaze. Then Theagenes beat his head, tore his hair, and cried aloud: "Farewell to life this day! fears, dangers, anxieties, hope, and love— all are ended; Chariclea is dead, Theagenes is undone. My cowardice has been of no avail to me; in vain did I flee from the battlefield in flight unworthy of a man, to save myself for you, my dearest love!

No longer will I survive you, now that you are lying dead, not (which is hardest of all) in accordance with the common law of nature, nor having breathed your last in your lover's arms. Alas! you have been consumed by fire; some cruel god has substituted these flames for the bridal torches. Your beauty has perished from amongst men; your dead body does not even preserve the remains of your unadulterated charms. Oh, unutterable cruelty! Oh, most bitter spite of fortune! I have been denied the favour of a last embrace, of a last and lifeless kiss." II. With these words, he would have grasped his sword, when Cnemon suddenly caught hold of him and thrust back his hand, crying out: "What is the meaning of this, Theagenes? why lament for her who is still alive? Chariclea is safe; take heart." "This tale is only fit for fools and children," replied Theagenes; "you have crowned my woes, by depriving me of a most delightful death." Thereupon Cnemon swore that his words were true and told the whole story; the instructions that Thyamis had given him, how he had let Chariclea down into the cave, and the formation of the same, which prevented all danger of the fire reaching the bottom, since it would be checked by the countless windings and turnings. At these words, Theagenes breathed again and hastened to the island, in his mind already seeing Chariclea and representing to himself the cave as his nuptial chamber, ignorant what sorrow awaited him there.

They advanced in all haste, being obliged to row themselves; for their boatman, at the beginning of the engagement, struck by the first shouts of the enemy, as if by a swine-goad,1 had fallen overboard. Being little skilled in handling their oars and rowing together, they were carried backwards and forwards out of the straight course, while they also had to contend against an adverse wind. Nevertheless, their eagerness overcame their want of skill.

III. When, therefore, with great difficulty and effort they had at last reached the island, they hastened with all speed to the huts, which they found already con 1 The meaning of rWA.ij£ in this passage is very doubtful. 10 sumed by the fire, and only recognisable by the site which they had once occupied. The stone, however, which had formed the entrance to the cave was clearly to be seen; for a violent wind blowing upon the huts, that were only made of thin reeds and sedge intertwined, had fanned the flames in passing, and caused their total conflagration, exposing an almost level plain beneath. The flame, when it was extinguished, had left nothing but a heap of ashes, most of which had been carried away by the violence of the wind, while the few that remained, although still smouldering, had cooled sufficiently to allow anyone to pass over. Having found some half-lighted torches and kindled some fragments of reeds, they opened the mouth of the cave and hastened down, Cnemon going first. But, after they had proceeded a little way, he suddenly cried out: "O Jove! what means this? We are lost; Chariclea is no more!" With these words, he let the torch fall from his hands, and it went out; he himself, clasping his hands before his eyes, sank on his knees, weeping bitterly. But Theagenes, as if urged forward by some irresistible force, fell upon the body of the woman lying on the ground, and for a long time, motionless, held it clasped in a close embrace. Cnemon, seeing that he was utterly overwhelmed with grief and bathed in sorrow, was afraid that he might make an attempt upon his life. Secretly drawing his sword, which hung by his side, from its scabbard, he left him to himself, and ran out to light his torch again. IV. In the meanwhile, Theagenes filled the cavern with his loud and mournful wailing: "Oh, grief unbearable! oh, calamity sent upon me from heaven! what insatiable fury rages for our destruction, and has driven us

from our country, exposed us to dangers on sea and the attacks of pirates, often delivered us into the hands of brigands, and robbed us of all our possessions? One comfort alone remained to me; now, even this has been taken from me. Chariclea lies dead, and she who was dearer than all to me has been destroyed by the hand of the enemy, doubtless in defence of her chastity, to preserve it for me. Now the unhappy woman lies dead, having reaped no benefit from her beauty, without my having enjoyed it myself. Oh, my dearest, bid me a last farewell; give me your last commands, if the breath of life is still in you. Alas! you are silent. Those heavenly and prophetic lips are hushed in silence; the shades of darkness have enveloped the bearer of the torch and chaos the priestess of the gods. Those eyes which charmed all with their beauty are closed for ever. I am convinced your murderer never saw them. But by what name am I to call you? my betrothed? But you have never been betrothed. My wife? But you never knew the meaning of the word. What, then, am I to call you? How shall I address you for the last time? By the sweetest name of all — Chariclea? Oh, Chariclea, be of good cheer; you have a faithful lover; soon you shall see me again. I will celebrate your obsequies by my own death and offer to you a libation of my own blood that is so dear to you. This cave shall be our impromptu tomb. In it we shall at least be united after death, although, during our lifetime, this has been denied us."

V. With these words, he stretched out his hand to draw his sword; but not finding it, he exclaimed: "Oh, Cnemon, you have destroyed me, and again wronged Chariclea, having a second time deprived her of the company of him who was her greatest delight."

While he was thus speaking, the sound of a voice came from the inmost recesses of the cave, crying out, "Theagenes." In no wise troubled, he heard and answered: "My dearest, I will come. It is evident that your shade still wanders upon earth; methinks you cannot endure to quit that body from which you were driven by force, or, being yet unburied, are perhaps refused admittance to the company of the shades below." In the meantime, Cnemon had returned with his torch relighted, when the same voice was heard again, calling "Theagenes." "Good heavens!" exclaimed Cnemon, "is that not the voice of Chariclea that I hear? I believe she is still alive, Theagenes; for the voice that has just struck my ear proceeds from the inmost recesses of the cave, where I remember that I left her." "Oh, Cnemon," said Theagenes, "will you never cease to deceive me?" "Well, if I deceive you, I am myself deceived; let us see whether this corpse be really Chariclea." With these words, he turned the body on its back, and, looking at it attentively, exclaimed: "Oh, ye gods! what prodigy is this? This is the face of Thisbe!" Then he stepped back, and stood trembling and motionless, like one dumbfounded.

VI. But Theagenes, who now began to breathe again, with hope revived, called upon Cnemon, who seemed ready to faint, and begged him to lead him with all speed to Chariclea. After a little time, Cnemon recovered, and again examined the corpse, and saw that it was really Thisbe; by her side lay a sword, which he recognised by its hilt as belonging to Thyamis, who, in his mad frenzy, had left it in the wound. Seeing a letter in Thisbe's bosom, he took it out, and would have read it, but Theagenes would not permit him to do so, and earnestly pressed him, saying: "Let us first recover our dear Char idea; who knows whether some god is even now mocking us; we shall be able to read the letter afterwards." Cnemon consenting, they took up the letter and the sword, and hastened to Chariclea, who, dragging herself on her hands and knees in the direction of the light, threw her arms round her lover's neck. "Oh, Theagenes, do I really hold you in my arms?" "Oh, Chariclea, are you still preserved to me?" This they kept repeating, until, at last, they suddenly fell upon the ground, clinging to each other, fast entangled in their embraces, and unable to utter a word. It seemed as if death had overtaken them; for oftentimes excess of joy ends in sorrow, and immoderate pleasure begets pain, which we have brought upon ourselves. Thus these two lovers, preserved beyond their hopes, seemed at death's door, until Cnemon, by scraping the rock, discovered a tiny stream of running water, under which he held his hands, caught some of the slowly falling drops, and, dashing them in their faces and moistening their nostrils from time to time, gradually revived them. VII. Theagenes and Chariclea, finding themselves in each other's arms, started up blushing (especially Chariclea) at the thought that they had thus abandoned themselves to their extravagant transports in the presence of Cnemon, and besought him to pardon their excesses. Cnemon, gently smiling, restored their cheerfulness. "Nay, your behaviour deserves praise in my opinion, and in the opinion of every man who has entered the lists with love, has felt the pleasure of being vanquished by him, and made acquaintance, but in moderation, with his inevitable accidents. But there are other things, of which I can by no means approve, Theagenes; I was really ashamed to see you embrace a strange woman who was in no way known to you, and weeping over the body of a slave, especially when I protested to you that the object of your affections was still alive." "Oh, Cnemon," replied Theagenes, "cease to slander me to Chariclea; it was she whom I was lamenting in the person of another; it was her body that I thought I was watering with my tears. But, since some kindly Deity has opened my eyes and shown me my mistake, it is time for you to remember the great bravery which led you first to deplore my misfortunes, and, when you suddenly came upon the dead body, made you, a brave Athenian warrior, armed from head to foot, with your drawn sword in your hand, run away from a woman—and a dead woman, too—like the actors from the devils on the stage." VIII. At this they smiled slightly, but a forced smile, and not without tears, which were rather tears of grief, caused by the magnitude of their calamity. After a brief interval, Chariclea, gently passing her hand over her cheek, as if in thought, said: "I es-

teem her happy, whoever she may be, whom Theagenes lamented and even kissed! Do not think me jealous, if I ask you to tell me who was the happy woman, who was honoured by the tears of Theagenes, and how you came и to be so deceived as to kiss her as if she had been myself: if you know, I wish you would tell me." "You will be surprised," replied Theagenes; "Cnemon here declares that it is Thisbe, the Athenian lute-player, who contrived the plots against Demaeneta and himself." Chariclea, astounded at what she heard, said: "But how could she have been transported, as if by enchantment, from the midst of Greece to the furthest bounds of Egypt? and how was it that we did not see her when we came hither?" "That I cannot tell you," answered Cnemon; "all I know is this. When Demaeneta, finding herself tricked, flung herself into the pit, my father informed the people of what had happened, and was immediately acquitted; after which he endeavoured to secure my recall from banishment, and made preparations to set sail in search of me. In the meantime Thisbe, taking advantage of the leisure which her master's occupation afforded her, frequented all the festivals, at which she shamelessly prostituted her art and person. One day, having outdone Arsinoe, who had sung somewhat slowly and loosely, whereas she swept the strings rapidly and sang a delightful air, she drew upon herself, without knowing it, all the jealousy and hatred of which a courtesan is capable. This jealousy was increased when a wealthy merchant from Naucratis, by name Nausicles, embraced Thisbe, spurning Arsinoe, who had formerly been his mistress, because, while she was playing, he saw her cheeks puffed out, and, in consequence of her violent blowing, protruding most unbecomingly as far as her nose, while her flaming eyes seemed ready to start out of her head.

IX. "Arsinoe, swelling with rage and inflamed with jealousy, went and informed Demaeneta's relatives of Thisbe's intrigues against her mistress, some of which she had herself suspected, and had learnt the rest from Thisbe while they had been intimate. Demaeneta's relatives accordingly conspired against my father, and bribed the most famous orators to accuse him. They asserted that Demaeneta had perished without having been judged or condemned; that the charge of adultery was only a pretext invented to excuse her murder; and they demanded that the supposed adulterer should be produced, alive or dead, or that, at least, his name should be given; lastly, they claimed that Thisbe should be handed over to them, that she might be put to the torture. My father promised, but was unable to produce her; for Thisbe, foreseeing what would happen, even before the process was drawn up, had taken flight with the merchant, by previous arrangement. The people, although highly indignant, did not indeed judge my father to be the murderer of his wife, for he had told them all that had taken place, but expelled him from the city as an accessory to the plot against Demaeneta and to the unjust sentence of banishment against myself, and confiscated his property. Such were the fruits of his second marriage; and this was how Thisbe, that vilest of women, came to leave Athens, and, as we see, paid the penalty of her crimes.

"Such are the facts which I heard from one Anticles in Aegina, with whom I set sail again for Egypt, to see whether I could find Thisbe in Naucratia, take her back to Athens, and so dispel the suspicions and accusations directed against my father, and at the same time exact vengeance from this woman for her treachery against us all. But now I am here with you. Another time you shall learn the cause and manner of my captivity, and my misfortunes during the interval. But how Thisbe came into this cave and by whom she was slain, we shall need some god to tell us.

X. "But let us now examine the letter which we found in her bosom; it is probable that it will afford us further information." His suggestion being approved of, he opened the note, and read as follows:

"TO MY MASTER CNEMON, FROM HIS ENEMY AND AVENGER, THISBE.

"First, let me announce to you the welcome news of Demaeneta's death; it is I who have avenged you. If you will receive me, I will tell you the circumstances of her death in person. In the next place, I have been for ten days in this island, taken prisoner by one of the brigands, who boasts that he is the captain's armour-bearer, and keeps me shut up, not even permitting me to peep out of the door; he declares that he acts thus from his friendship for me; but I myself suspect he is afraid that I may be carried off by some one else. But, by the mercy of some god, oh, my master! I saw you passing by and recognised you; and now I am secretly sending you this letter by an old woman who lives with me, having charged her to give it into the hands of the handsome Greek, the captain's friend. Rescue me, I beg you, from the brigand's hands, and receive your handmaid. If you will, save my life; remember that, when I seemed to wrong you, I was compelled to do so; but that, when I avenged you, I acted on my own impulse. But, if your resentment is so violent that it cannot be appeased, employ it against me as you please. I am ready even for death, if only I may die yours. For I consider it far better to die by your hands and to ob tain the rights of burial according to the custom of Greece, than to endure a life more terrible even than death, and the love of a barbarian more odious to me than the hatred of an Athenian." XI. Such was the contents of Thisbe's letter. Then said Cnemon: "Oh Thisbe! you did well to die; and now you yourself are the messenger of your misfortunes, delivering into our hands after death this letter that tells the story of them. It seems that some avenging fury, driving you from one country to another, never stayed the lash of justice until she brought me, your injured master, although I was in Egypt, to be the spectator of your punishment. But what new stratagem were you plotting against me by this letter, when fortune cut you off before the attempt? Even in death I cannot help suspecting you, and I greatly fear that even Demaeneta's death may be a fiction, and that those

who told me news of it may have deceived me. How do I know that you did not come across the sea to play upon the stage of Egypt a tragedy similar to that which you played in Athens?" "What!" said Theagenes, "still so brave and bold? are you still afraid of ghosts and shadows? I have nothing to do with the drama that has ended thus; you cannot say that she has bewitched me and my eyesight. Believe me, Thisbe is really dead; you have nothing more to fear from her. But, who has done you this kindness, whose hand has slain her, how and when she came here, this perplexes and astonishes me." "I am as ignorant as yourself," said Cnemon; "but it was Thyamis who killed her, if we may conjecture from the sword, which we found lying by the victim's side; I recognise it as his by the ivory eagle carved upon the hilt." "But can you say when, how, and why he committed this crime?" "How should I know? This cave has not bestowed upon me the gift of divination, like the Delphic shrine or the cave of Trophonius, which are said to inspire with prophetic frenzy those who enter them." At these words, Theagenes and Chariclea suddenly began to weep and wail, crying out, "Oh Pytho! Oh Delphi!" This amazed Cnemon, who could not imagine why the name of Pytho should have thus affected them.

XII. Such were the fortunes of Cnemon, Theagenes, and Chariclea. While they were thus engaged, Thermuthis, Thyamis's armour-bearer, who had been wounded in the engagement, had managed to swim ashore. When night came on, having found one of the shipwrecked barks drifting about the marsh, he got into it and directed his course towards the island in search of Thisbe; for it was he who, a few days before, had carried her off by a sudden attack, when she was being conducted by Nausicles, the merchant, through a narrow pass at the foot of the mountain. In the midst of the disturbance caused by the approach of the enemy, he had taken advantage of the instructions given him by Thyamis to go in search of a victim, to put Thisbe under shelter, in order to keep her unhurt for himself. But, while letting her down into the cavern, in his hurry and confusion he had unawares left her at the entrance. Fright, the imminence of danger, want of familiarity with the winding passages which led to the bottom, kept her fixed to the spot where he had left her, so that Thyamis, finding her there, slew her in mistake for Chariclea. It was in search of her that Thermuthis was hurrying, thinking that he had escaped the dangers of war. As soon as he reached the island, he hastened towards the huts, which he found in ashes. Having with difficulty recognised the entrance to the cave by the stone that formed its covering, he lighted a handful of reeds which were left, and hastened down, calling Thisbe by her name in Greek. When he saw her stretched upon the ground, he stood for a long time dazed, unable to speak. At last, he heard sounds and a kind of murmur proceeding from the recesses of the cave; for Theagenes and Cnemon were still talking together. He had no doubt that they were Thisbe's murderers; but his perplexity was great, and he did not know what to make up his mind to do; the ferocity natural to brigands and the rage of a barbarian, aggravatedat the moment by the disappointment of his desires, urged him to rush headlong upon those whom he believed to be the authors of the murder; but, on the other hand, the want of a sword or other arms obliged him to restrain himself, though much against his will. XIII. It seemed to him that the best plan would be to go to meet them, without at first showing signs of any hostile intent; and then, if he could by any means procure arms, to attack them as enemies. Having resolved upon this, he directed his steps towards Theagenes, throwing round him wild and savage glances, and revealing in his looks the hidden purpose of his soul. At the sudden appearance of this stranger, naked and wounded, with his face covered with blood, Chariclea withdrew into the interior of the cave, partly in alarm, but partly also from a feeling of modesty at the hideous sight of this naked stranger. Cnemon also quietly drew back a little; he had recognised Thermuthis, but was surprised at his sudden appearance, and was afraid that he might do something desperate. Theagenes, on the other hand, irritated rather than alarmed, pointed his sword at him, as if he intended to stab him at the first indication of hostility. "Stop," he cried, "or you will suffer for it; if I have spared you, it is because I recognised you, and I am not yet sure with what purpose you are come." Then Thermuthis, forced by necessity rather than his natural inclinations to become a suppliant, fell at his feet and asked for pardon. At the same time, he called upon Cnemon to help him, saying that he deserved succour from him; that he had never done him any injury, that he had fought by his side on the previous day, and that he now came to them as to friends. XIV. Cnemon was touched by his entreaties; he went up to Thermuthis, who was still clasping the knees of Theagenes, lifted him up, and asked him eagerly where Thyamis was. Thermuthis told him all he knew about him; how he had attacked the enemy, how he had plunged into the thickest of the fight, without thought of their lives or his own; how he had slain all who came in his way, being himself protected by the general order that he was to be taken alive. He declared that he did not know what had been Thyamis's fate; for, having been wounded himself, he had swum to land, and was now come in search of Thisbe. When they asked him what interest he could have in Thisbe, why he sought her, and how she had come into his possession, he told them the whole story; how he had taken her away from the merchants, how he had fallen violently in love with her, how he had kept her hidden in his tent, and, on the approach of the enemy, had let her down into the cave, where he had just found her lying dead, slain by an unknown hand; he added that he was very eager to find out who had committed the murder, and what had been their motives. Cnemon, being exceedingly anxious to free himself from all suspicion, told him that Thyamis was the murderer, in proof of which he showed him the sword that had been found near the dead body.

When Thermuthis saw it, still dripping with blood, the blade still warm from the recently-inflicted wound, and recognised it as the property of Thyamis, he uttered a deep sigh, and, not knowing how to account for what had taken place, in a state of gloomy stupor made his way back to the entrance to the cave. When he came to the body of Thisbe, he placed his head upon her breast, and, continually repeating nothing but the name of Thisbe, at first the name in full, then, more slowly, syllable by syllable, at last he fell asleep. XV. Theagenes, Chariclea and Cnemon, reflecting upon all that had taken place, began to deliberate what was best for them to do; but the multitude of their past calamities, their present sufferings and embarrassments, and the uncertainty of the future, obscured their reasoning powers. At every moment, they looked at each other, each of them waiting for the other to propose something; then, being disappointed, they bent their eyes upon the ground, lifted them up again, took breath, and lightened their grief by deepdrawn sighs. At length, Cnemon threw himself upon the ground. Theagenesflung himself upon a rock, and Chariclea reclined upon his breast. For some time they struggled against the attacks of sleep, being anxious, if they could, to devise some plan; but at length, overcome by fatigue and exhaustion, they submitted, although against their will, to the call of nature, and fell into a refreshing slumber from very excess of sorrow. Thus the intelligent part of the soul is sometimes obliged to sympathise with and yield to the fatigues of the body. XVI. But, almost as soon as they had closed their eyelids and snatched a few moments of sleep, Chariclea, lying upon Theagenes's bosom, had a dream. A man with dishevelled hair, a gloomy and savage look, and bloody hands, seemed to thrust out her right eye with a sword. She immediately cried out, declaring that her eye had been pulled out, and called upon Theagenes for help. When he heard her call, he immediately hastened up to her, being deeply affected himself, as if, while he was asleep, a kind of sympathy had made him share her suffering. She had lifted her hand to her face, as if feeling everywhere for the part which she had lost in her vision; then, understanding that it was only a dream, she exclaimed: "I was dreaming; my eye is safe; fear nothing, Theagenes. " At these words, he breathed again: "It is well that no harm has befallen those bright rays of the sun; but, tell me what has happened, what caused your sudden alarm?" "A fierce and savage man, not even fearing your invincible might, attacked me with a sword as I lay at your feet, and, as it seemed to me, struck out my right eye; and would to Heaven that it had been a reality rather than a dream." "Heaven forbid!" said Theagenes; "why do you wish that?" "It would be better for me to lose one ot my eyes than to be anxious about you. I am greatly afraid that this dream has reference to you—you whom I look upon as my eyes, my life, my all." "Do not say that," interrupted Cnemon, who had heard everything, having been awakened by Chariclea's cries: "I can give another interpretation to the dream; tell me, are your parents living?" "Yes," she replied,

"and if they were ""Then believe that your father lives no longer; this I conjecture for the following reason. We know that our parents are the authors of our life, and that it is owing to them that we see the light of the day: therefore, the comparison of our father and mother to our two eyes, as being the sense capable of light, and the means whereby we discern things visible, seems to me a natural one." "A grievous misfortune is this you announce," said Chariclea; "but may this interpretation prove true rather than the other; may your oracle be verified, and may I be shown a false prophet." "The event will show the truth of my prediction," said Cnemon, "and you must rest content. But methinks we are really dreaming, while we trouble ourselves about dreams and vain imaginations, instead of taking advantage of the opportunity to consider what is best for us to do, while this Egyptian (meaning Thermuthis) has left us, to mourn for his dead mistress?" XVII. Theagenes, taking him up, said: "Oh, Cnemon! since some god has united you to us and made you the partner of all our misfortunes, do you give your advice first. You know the neighbourhood and understand the language of the country. Overwhelmed with greater calamities than you, we are less in a condition to understand what is best to do." After a few moments' silence, Cnemon spoke as follows: "We do not know which of us is the most unfortunate; Heaven has laid upon me also a heavy burden of woes; yet, since you desire that I, as being the eldest, should give my advice first, I will do as you wish. This island, as you see, is deserted, and we are its only inhabitants. It contains abundance of gold, silver, and stuffs; for in this cave are stored the treasures which Thyamis has taken from you and many others; but it is absolutely destitute of corn and all the necessaries of life. If we stay here longer, we run the risk of perishing from hunger, or at the hands of the enemy, should they return, or even of our own comrades, should they rally and come back for the sake of the treasures, of the existence and whereabouts of which they cannot be ignorant. Then we should be unable to escape death; or, even should they treat us more leniently, we should be exposed to insults and outrages at their hands. These men1 are rarely to be trusted, and especially when they have no leader to restrain them and check their violence. We must therefore leave this island, and shun it as if it were a prison or a net; but we must first get rid of Thermuthis, under pretence of sending him to try if he can find out what has become of Thyamis. We shall be able to deliberate more at our ease if we are alone; and shall more readily carry into execution what we decide to do. Besides, it is better in any case to get this man out of the way; for he is by nature quarrelsome and savage, and not to be depended upon; he also suspects us of being Thisbe's murderers, and will not rest until he has made an attempt upon our lives, should he ever have the opportunity." XVIII. The others approved of Cnel *Literaljy,* "cowherds." mon's advice and resolved to follow it. Perceiving that it was day, they hastened to

the mouth of the cave, and woke Thermuthis, who was in a deep sleep; they informed him of their resolution, but only told him so much as it was absolutely necessary for him to know; and he, being of a credulous disposition, readily believed what they said. They then dug a pit, in which they deposited the body of Thisbe, covered it with the ashes, the sole remains of the huts that had been burnt, and rendered the last rites to it, as well as they were able and as far as time permitted, watering the grave with tears in place of libations; after which, they despatched Thermuthis on the errand agreed upon. But he had only gone a few steps, when he turned back, declaring that he would not go alone, that he would not undertake so dangerous a search by himself, unless Cnemon would consent to accompany him. Theagenes, when he saw that Cnemon was afraid (for, when Thermuthis's request was explained to him, he was evidently greatly alarmed), said: "What, Cnemon! so strong in counsel, and so weak in execution! Your present behaviour confirms my previous opinion of you. Come, recall your courage, pluck up your spirits. You must consent and accompany him at first, lest your refusal should make him suspect our design of flight. You are armed and carry a sword; what have you to fear from one who is unarmed? At the first favourable opportunity you can steal away from him and rejoin us at a place we will settle upon; let this be some neighbouring village, the inhabitants of which are kindly disposed." Cnemon approved of this suggestion, and mentioned a town called Chemmis, flourishing and populous, situated near the banks of the Nile, upon a hill, to defend it against the incursions of robbers. This town, after crossing the lake, is distant about a hundred stades, due south.

XIX. "That is a difficult matter," replied Theagenes, "at least for Chariclea, who is not accustomed to long journeys; however, we will go, and pretend that we are beggars, some of those jugglers who get their living from what the public bestow upon them." "Very good, by Hercules!" said Cnemon; "you are sufficiently ugly and deformed, especially Chariclea, who has just had her eye knocked out; from your present appearance, however, you seem to me to be candidates not for 'the crumbs, but for the knives and plates.'" At these words, he smiled slightly, but with a forced smile, which did not go beyond the lips. Having confirmed their agreement by an oath, they called the gods to witness that they would never desert one another, and commenced to put their plan into execution. Cnemon and Thermuthis, having crossed the lake early in the morning, made their way with difficulty through a dense wood. Thermuthis led the way, at the suggestion of Cnemon, on the pretence that, as the road was difficult and Thermuthis was more familiar with it, it would be better for him to act as guide; in reality he was thinking of his own safety and was looking for an opportunity of running away. As they went on, they fell in with some flocks, whose keepers fled at their approach, and concealed themselves in the thickest part of the forest. They seized one of the choicest rams, cut its throat, broiled it over a fire which the shepherds had lighted, and, being violently hungry, eagerly devoured the flesh, without waiting until it was properly cooked. Like wolves and jackals, they tore off and swallowed large pieces, hardly warmed through; the blood of the half-cooked flesh trickled down their mouths as they gorged themselves with it. After they had satisfied their hunger, they quenched their thirst with milk, and resumed their journey. In the evening, while they were ascending a hill, Thermuthis declared that there was a village at the foot of it, where it was probable that Thyamis was being kept prisoner, if indeed he had not been killed. Then Cnemon began to complain of pains in his stomach; he said that he had eaten too heartily, and that the milk had given him violent diarrhoea. He begged Thermuthis to go on ahead, saying that he would catch him up. He did the same two or three times, but his companion suspected nothing, and believed that he really had great difficulty in keeping up with him. XX. When he had accustomed the Egyptian to his staying behind, he at last waited a considerable time; and then, plunging into the thickest part of the forest, ran downhill as fast as he could. When Thermuthis had reached the top of the hill, he sat down upon a rock, waiting for the approach of night; for it had been agreed between them that they should wait until it was dark, before they entered the town to make enquiries about Thyamis. At the same time, he looked about to see whether there were any signs of Cnemon, against whom he had evil designs; for, as he still suspected that it was he who had killed Thisbe, he was thinking how he might treat him in like manner; in his furious rage, he even had an idea of killing Theagenes afterwards. However, finding that Cnemon did not appear, as the night was now far advanced, Thermuthis fell asleep—a deadly and last sleep for him; for an asp, no doubt guided by the will of Fate, bit him and put a fitting end to his life.

Cnemon, from the moment he had left Thermuthis, continued his flight without taking breath, until night and darkness compelled him to halt. He hid himself in the place where night had surprised him, gathered together as many leaves as he could, and covered himself with them. But he scarcely slept, being a prey to mortal dread. At the slightest noise, at the least breath of wind, at the rustling of the leaves, he fancied that he heard Thermuthis. If sleep sometimes overcame him for a moment, he thought that he was fleeing; that he was turning round every instant to look behind and discover an enemy who had no existence. Although he wanted to sleep, he resisted its approach, in order to escape from the dreams which were more terrible than even the reality itself. At last, he vented his irritation upon the night, which appeared to him longer than usual. At length, to his great joy, daylight appeared. At first, being afraid of frightening those whom he might meet, or of arousing their suspicions, he cut his hair, which he had allowed to grow while he was with the shepherds, in order to give himself the appearance of a brigand. For these people, amongst oth-

er devices for making themselves look as terrible as possible, comb their hair down over their eyebrows and let it grow down over their shoulders; for they know well that, while a flowing head of hair adds grace to the lover, it makes the brigand look more terrible.

XXI. When he had cut his hair after the fashion of ordinary individuals, he hastened towards Chemmis, the meeting-place agreed upon with Theagenes. When he reached the Nile and was about to cross over to Chemmis, he saw an old man wandering upon the banks, hastily walking up and down, as if he were holding communication with the river. His hair, which he wore long like the priests, was as white as snow; his long, thick beard gave him a venerable aspect; his cloak and the rest of his garments resembled those of the Greeks. Cnemon stopped for a moment; the old man kept passing backwards and forwards in front of him, as if he did not notice that there was anyone there, so entirely absorbed was he in his thoughts and wrapt in meditation. Cnemon then accosted him with the words: "Hail! be of good cheer." "There is no more joy for me," replied the old man, "my fortune forbids it." Cnemon, in surprise, asked: "Are you a Greek or a foreigner, or what is your native country?" "I am neither a Greek nor a foreigner, but an Egyptian, a native of this country." "Why, then, do you wear this Greek dress?" "It is my misfortune that has clothed me in these splendid garments. " Cnemon, being unable to understand how misfortune could improve a man's attire, seemed desirous of hearing his story. "You are carrying me out of Ilium," said the old man, "and are stirring up a swarm of evils, which will assail you with perpetual buzzing. But whence come you, young man, and whither are you going? How comes it that you, in Egypt, speak the Greek language?" "Your request is unreasonable," said Cnemon; "you have told me nothing about yourself, although I asked you first, and now you want to know my story." "Very well, then," replied the old man, " I will not refuse; for you seem to me to be a Greek, in spite of the disguise which some caprice of Fortune has imposed upon you. Besides, if you are so eager to learn my history, I myself am terribly anxious to recount it; probably I should have told it to these reeds, like Midas in the fable, if I had not met you. But let us leave the Nile and its banks; a spot that is scorched by the noonday sun is by no means suitable for hearing a long story. Let us go to the town which you see on the other side, right opposite here, unless more important business prevents you. 1 can offer you hospitality, not at my own house, but at that of a worthy man who has received me as a suppliant; there, you shall hear the story of my misfortunes, if you so desire, and shall confide to me your own in return." "Let us go," said Cnemon; "in fact, I myself am going to this very town, to wait for some friends, with whom I have an appointment." XXII. They got into one of the numerous boats that were lying off the bank, ready to take passengers across for a fee, and directed their course towards the town. When they reached the house where the old man had found shelter, the master of the house was absent; but his daughter, a tall, well-grown girl, together with the servants of the household, gave them a cordial welcome. They treated the old man as if he had been their father, having probably been bidden to do so by their master. One washed his feet, and wiped off the dust which covered his legs; another looked after his bed, and strewed it with soft coverlets. One brought water and lighted a fire; another set bread and all fruits of the season upon the table.

Cnemon, astonished at all this, exclaimed: "It seems to me, father, that we have entered the abode of Jove the God of Hospitality, so unhesitating is the attention and so remarkable the kindness with which we have been received." "It is not the house of Jove," he replied, "but that of a man who reveres Jove the God of Hospitality, the protector of suppliants. He also, my son, leads a wandering life; he is a merchant, and with his own eyes has made acquaintance with many cities, and with the manners and the minds of many men. This is doubtless the reason why he has received under his roof so many other unfortunates like myself, who but a few days ago was a homeless vagabond." "And how, then, came you to be a wanderer?" "The brigands have taken away my children; I know those who have carried them off, but I am unable to punish them. This is why I roam about this spot, pursuing my misfortune with my grief. In like manner a bird, when a serpent attacks its nest, and devours its little ones before its eyes, fears to approach, and yet cannot resign itself to flight; love and fear struggle for mastery; it circles with mournful cries round the nest which is in the enemy's possession, and pours its maternal wailings and useless supplications into barbarous ears which nature has made deaf to all feelings of pity." "Tell me, then," said Cnemon, ' how and when you have had to undergo this painful struggle." "I will do so later; in the meantime, we must look after our stomachs; it was a wonderfully happy expression on Homer's part, to call the belly 'destructive,' since it puts itself before everything else. And first, according to the custom of the Egyptian sages, let us pour libations to the gods. Nothing will ever make me neglect to do this; no misfortune, however great, will ever have power to make me forget what I owe to the gods." XXIII. With these words, he poured pure water (this was his only drink) out of the cup, saying: "I pour this libation to the gods of the country and to those of Greece; also to you, oh Pythian Apollo, and to you, Theagenes and Chariclea, good and virtuous children; for you also I reckon amongst the number of the gods." At the same time he shed tears, as it were by way of a second libation. Cnemon, when he heard these names, was struck with astonishment, and looked at the old man from head to foot: "What do you say?" he exclaimed; "are Theagenes and Chariclea your children?" "They are my children, oh stranger, although they were not given to me by a mother; Fortune and the will of the gods have made them mine; the travail of my soul has brought them forth; my affection for them has taken

the place of the ties of kinship; thanks to this affection, they look upon me as their father, and call me by that name. But, tell me, how do you come to know them?" "I not only know them," replied Cnemon, "but I tell you the good news that they are alive." "Oh Apollo, and all ye other gods!" exclaimed the old man; "where are they? Speak, and I will look upon you as my preserver and the equal of the gods." "And what shall be my reward?" "For the moment, my gratitude, the best of all rewards in the eyes of a man who is wise; I know many who have laid up this as a treasure in their hearts. Afterwards, when we have returned to my country— and this, so the gods foretell, will not be long—you shall draw as much wealth as you please from my store." "These are vague and uncertain promises; you have it in your power to reward me on the spot." "Speak, if you see anything that I can offer you now; I would willingly sacrifice even one of my limbs." "There is no need of so great a sacrifice; I shall consider myself fully repaid, if you tell me whence they come, who were their parents, how they came here, and what their fortunes have been." "You shall have a reward second to none, even though you should ask for all the wealth of the universe. But, first of all, let us take some food; for you will have a long tale to listen to, and I shall have much to say." They then ate a few nuts, figs, fresh dates, and other fruits of this kind, which formed the old man's usual food; for he never deprived any animal of its life to provide food for himself; his drink was water, while Cnemon took some wine. After a brief interval of silence, Cnemon said: "You know, father, that Bacchus delights in convivial tales and songs. He has this day claimed my hospitality; he has aroused in me a desire to listen to you, and urges me to claim my promised reward; it is time for you to put your piece upon the stage, as the saying is." "Listen then," said the old man; "and would to Heaven that the worthy Nausicles were here, for he has often entreated me to tell him this story, but has always been put off under some pretext or another." stopped as if to check himself. When the old man asked what was the matter with him, Cnemon, in order to put him off the scent, replied that he was greatly surprised, and wondered with what forces he intended to attack them. "The satrap of the great king in Egypt is Oroondates, under whose orders Mitranes is in command of the garrison of this town. Nausicles, by means of a large sum of money, has persuaded the latter to assist him with a large number of soldiers, foot and horse. He is especially annoyed at the loss of this Greek girl, not only because he really loved her and she was a clever musician, but also because he was going to take her with him to the King of Aethiopia, to be companion of the queen's amusements, and her associate according to the usage of the Greeks. Finding himself thus disappointed of the considerable profit which he expected to make by her, he is doing his very utmost to get her back again. I myself have encouraged him in the undertaking, in the idea that he might perhaps meet my children somewhere and restore them to me." "Enough of shepherds, satraps, and kings," said Cnemon; "you have wandered from the point, and nearly transported me at the very outset to the end of the story. This episode is brought in rather unnaturally, and has nothing to do with Bacchus, as the phrase goes; you are like Proteus of Pharos, with the difference that, instead of changing yourself into false and fleeting shapes, you are trying to lead me away from the subject." "Well, then, you shall hear all," replied the old man; "but I will first give you a rapid account of myself, not in order, as you imagine, to throw dust in your eyes, but in order to prepare you for a connected and well-arranged narrative of later events. I was born at Memphis; my father's name, like my own, was Calasiris. Although I now lead a wandering life, a short time ago I filled the office of high priest. I took a wife, according to the custom of the country; I lost her, according to the law of nature. When, released from the trammels of this life, she had entered XXIV. "And where may he be now?" asked Cnemon, as soon as he heard the name of Nausicles mentioned. "He is gone hunting," replied the old man. "After what kind of game?" "Wild beasts, the most savage in existence; they are called men and shepherds; in reality, they are brigands by profession, and are most difficult to catch; for they live in a marsh instead of lairs and caves." "And what injury have they done him?" "They have carried off from him an Athenian maiden whom he loved, who was called Thisbe." "Good heavens!" cried Cnemon, and then immediately the repose of another world, for some time I remained free from the blows of misfortune, delighting myself in the society of the two sons whom she had left me. But, a few years later, the fatal course of the celestial bodies upset my destiny; the eye of Saturn struck my house, and changed its fortunes for the worse. Wisdom revealed these ills to me, but without showing me the means of escaping them. For, although it is possible to foresee the immutable decrees of the Fates, it is useless to endeavour to avoid them. And yet foreknowledge is an advantage, at least relatively, since it blunts the edge of adversity. An unforeseen misfortune, my son, is intolerable; those which we know in advance are easier to bear; in the first case, the mind, seized with fear, is cast down; in the second, reflection familiarises it with the idea of them.

XXV. "The following is what happened to me: A Thracian woman, named Rhodopis, in the prime of life, as beautiful even as Chariclea, came to the country (I know not whence or how), to the ruin of those who became acquainted with her. After travelling through Egypt, she settled at Memphis. Her numerous suite, the magnificence she displayed, her charms, her cleverness in setting the snares of Venus—all this made it impossible for anyone to look upon her without being hopelessly bewitched. Never was there a courtesan who knew better how to attract a man with her irresistible fascinations. From time to time she visited the temple of Isis, of which I was priest, frequently consecrating to the goddess victims and sumptuous offerings. I must tell the

truth, although it makes me blush; the frequent sight of her overcame me; she gained the victory over the self-restraint which I had practised all my life. After I had for a long time resisted the eyes of the body with those of the mind, I at length succumbed, I fell overwhelmed by the weight of the burden of love. I saw in this woman the commencement of the misfortunes reserved for me by the gods, and which they had predicted; I foresaw in her the person of Destiny, and I under stood that she was the mask beneath which the evil Genius, in whose power I then was, lay concealed. Fearing to disgrace my sacred office, in which I had been brought up from infancy, I determined to avoid profaning the temple and sanctuary of the gods. I appointed reason my judge, and, punishing as it deserved the fault which I had committed—not in very deed, in truth, indeed (Heaven forbid!), but in desire—I imposed upon myself the penalty of exile. Unhappy that I was, I left my native land; I yielded to the irresistible power of the Fates, and gave myself up to them to deal with me as they pleased. I also wanted to escape from the accursed Rhodopis; for I was afraid that, still under the influence of my baleful star, I might be dragged into more disgraceful acts. But what, above all, made me decide to flee, was the fact that my skill in divination had several times foretold to me that my sons were destined to draw the sword against each other. I wished to tear my eyes away from so frightful a sight, in the presence of which even the sun would veil himself in a cloud to avoid being a witness of it. I spared the eyes of a father the sight of the murder of his children; I exiled myself from my country, from my father's house, without communicating my design to anyone. I had pretended that I was going to Egyptian Thebes, to see my eldest son, who was staying there on a visit to his grandfather. His name, oh stranger, was Thyamis." Cnemon started again, as if the name of Thyamis had struck him; but he restrained himself and kept silence to hear the continuation of the story. Calasiris proceeded: "I pass over in silence the intermediate part of my journey, which has nothing to do with what you want to know. XXVI. "Having heard that there was a city in Greece, named Delphi, consecrated to Apollo, and also that it was a sanctuary for all the other gods, and for the wise man a place of retirement1 far removed from popular disturbances, I directed my course thither; for it appeared to me that no place of refuge could be better suited for a priest than a city 1 Literally, "workshop." entirely devoted to religion and sacrifice. Having crossed the Gulf of Crissa, I landed at Cirrha, and, on disembarking, hastened up to the city. When I drew near to it, a voice, evidently divine, sounded in my ears; the city appeared to me in every respect, but especially from its natural situation, an abode worthy of no ordinary mortals. Parnassus, like a natural fortress, with a citadel which owes nothing to art, rises aloft, and throws out on one side and the other its spurs, which embrace as in its bosom the city lying at its feet." "Your description is most accurate," said Cnemon; "it seems to have been made by one who was really under the influence of the Pythian god; it tallies with that given me by my father, when he was sent as the deputy1 of the Athenian people to the Amphictyonic assembly." "So then you are an Athenian, my son?" "Yes." "What is your name?" "Cnemon." "What is your history?" "You shall hear it later; meanwhile, continue." "I will. I went up to the city, and, after having admired the race-courses,2 the 1 The *Hieromnemon* was the secretary sent by each of the twelve Amphictyonic states to their council together with the *Pylagoras* (the actual deputy or minister). 2 Or simply, "public walks." 16 market-places, and fountains (especially Castalia, with whose water I sprinkled myself), I hastened my steps towards the temple. The murmurs which announced that it was the hour when the priestess would be tinder the influence of the god, excited me greatly. Having entered the temple, I flung myself on the ground and uttered a silent prayer, and received the following oracle: 'Thou comest from the district of the fruitful Nile; thou fleest from the threads of the mighty Fates. Take heart; soon I will give thee the plains of Egypt with its dark furrows; meanwhile, be my friend.' XXVII. "As soon as I heard these prophetic words, I fell upon my face at the foot of the altar, and besought the god to be propitious to me in everything. The whole multitude of the bystanders glorified Apollo for the oracle which he had vouchsafed to me on the occasion of my first visit to the temple; they congratulated me, and treated me with particular respect, saying that I was the only man, with the exception of Lycurgus of Sparta, upon whom the god had bestowed the title of friend. They granted me permission to inhabit the precincts of the temple, at my request, and it was decreed that I should be maintained at the public expense. In short, my situation left nothing to be desired; I took part in the sacred ceremonies; I studied the numerous sacrifices of various kinds performed daily by strangers as well as natives, in honour of the god; I joined in the conversations of the philosophers who flocked in great numbers to the temple of the Pythian Apollo; for the city is really a sanctuary of the Muses, under the inspiration of the God whom the Muses recognise as their head. At the beginning, questions were put to me upon different subjects: one asked me in what manner we worshipped our gods in Egypt; another enquired why certain animals were worshipped in different places, and wanted an account of each; while others, again, put questions to me concerning the construction of the Pyramids and the underground burial-vaults of the kings; in a word, none of the curiosities of Egypt were forgotten, for everything relating to that country has a special charm for the Greeks. XXVIII. "At length, one of the most learned amongst them asked me about the Nile, its source, the special characteristics by which it 1s distinguished from other rivers, and why it is that it is the only river that overflows in summer. I told them what I knew on the subject, what I had gathered from the sacred books which the priests alone may read and consult. I told them that it rises in the

mountains of Aethiopia, on the furthest confines of Libya, where the east ends and the south begins. The reason of its overflowing in summer is not, as is sometimes asserted, that its waters are driven back by the Etesian winds, which blow in an opposite direction; but rather, these winds, at the period of the summer solstice, drive the clouds before them from north to south, until they collect beneath the torrid zone, where they are arrested in their course by the excessive heat of these regions; all the vapours previously accumulated gradually condense, are resolved into water, and fall in torrents of rain. The Nile swells, and, disdainfully overflowing its banks, is no longer a river, but a sea, which spreads over Egypt, and fertilises the plains over which it flows. This is the reason why its waters are so pleasant to drink, since they are composed of the rain from heaven, and are soft to the touch; although they are not so hot as they are at its source, they are nevertheless tepid. This explains why the Nile is the only river which exhales no vapours; whereas it would certainly do so, if it were true, as some learned men amongst the Greeks have asserted, that its rise is owing to the melting of the snows. XXIX. "While I was giving these explanations, the priest of Apollo, whose name was Charicles, and an intimate friend of mine, said to me: 'What you say is perfectly correct, and I am inclined to share your opinion, according to what I have heard from the priests of the Nile at the cataracts.' 'What!' said I to him, 'have you been there?' 'Yes,' he replied. 'And what necessity drove you thither?' 'A domestic misfortune, which turned out the cause of my happiness.' When I expressed my astonishment, he said: 'You will not be astonished when you hear how it happened; and you shall hear whenever you please.' 'You may speak at once,' I answered; 'I am ready to hear you.' 'Listen, then,' said Charicles, after he had dismissed the crowd; 'for I have long desired to confide to you the story of my adventures, and that from an interested motive.'

"'After my marriage I remained for a long time without children. At last, when I was advanced in years, the God, who had long been wearied by my supplications, permitted me to become the father of a girl, but at the same time predicted that I should have no reason to rejoice that she had been born. When she was old enough to be married, I gave her to the one of her numerous suitors whom I thought most worthy of her; but, the very night of her wedding, when she was in bed with her husband, the unhappy woman was burnt either by fire from heaven or by accident. The marriage-song, the strains of which had not yet ceased, was succeeded by lamentation; she passed from the marriage-chamber to the tomb, and the torches which had illuminated the wedding procession lighted up the funeral pile. To this tragic event the gods added a fresh misfortune; my wife succumbed to her grief. Incapable of resisting the misfortunes with which the Deity thus overwhelmed me, I would not, however, lay violent hands upon myself, so as not to disobey the interpreters of the divine law, who teach us that this is forbidden. I left my native land, and fled from the loneliness and desolation of my house. For nothing is better calculated to make us forget our misfortunes than to leave those objects the sight of which reawakens the sorrows of the soul. After having wandered through many countries, I also came to your Egypt and Catadupa,1 to visit the cataracts of the Nile.

XXX. "' Now that I have explained to you the reasons for my journey to Egypt, I must now enter upon a digression, 1 The name of the district of the Cataracts, as well as of the Cataracts themselves. although in reality it is my chief reason for telling my story. I was walking one day in the city, to occupy my time and buy some things which could not be procured in Greece (for time had by this time alleviated my excessive grief, and I was anxious to return to my own country), when I was accosted by a man of grave demeanour, whose look betokened shrewdness; his skin was perfectly black, and he had only just reached man's estate. He saluted me, and made me understand, in spite of the difficulty he found in expressing himself in Greek, that he had something to say to me. I willingly agreed to his request, and went with him into a temple in the neighbourhood. He then said to me: "I have seen you buying Indian, Aethiopian, and Egyptian roots and herbs; if you would like to buy some from me, at a fair price, without any cheating, I shall be happy to supply you. " "Well," said I, "let me see them." "You are sure to be satisfied, but do not be too hard upon me in regard to the price. " "Then you must not be too exorbitant in your de if you will agree to accept in addition an even still more valuable present." At these words I began to laugh, and, when he asked me the reason, I replied: "It seems to me absurd that, in order to make me accept these valuable gifts, you should offer me, as an inducement, a present of even greater value." "You may take my word," he said; "only you must swear, on your part, that you will make the best use of this gift, and will follow my instructions." In my astonishment, I hardly knew what to do; but at last I took an oath to him, allured by the hope of such vast wealth. When I had taken the oath, he led me to his house, and showed me a young girl of divine and incomparable beauty. He told me that she was only seven years of age, although she seemed to me old enough to marry, so much did her rare beauty seem to add to her stature. I stood mute with astonishment, unable to understand what it all meant, and enchanted by what I saw. mands." He then pulled out a small bag from under his arm, and showed me a quantity of precious stones of very great value. There were some diamonds as big as nuts, quite round, cut with most perfect skill, pure and sparkling; emeralds and sapphires,1 the one as green as the corn in spring, with the brilliant lustre of the olive, the other imitating the tints of the sea when it ruffles its surface slightly under shelter of an overhanging rock, and tinges with purple the objects beneath it. In a word, the stones were of varied brilliancy, and enchanted the eye. When I saw them, I said: "You had better find other purchasers for these; as

for me, all that I possess would scarcely be sufficient to pay for one of them. " "But, if it is not possible for you to buy them, you can at least receive them as a present." "Certainly; I am perfectly ready to receive them as a present, but I cannot understand why you are jesting with me." "I am not jesting," he replied; "I am in earnest; I swear by the god who presides over this temple that I will give all these stones, 1 The identity of these stones is a matter of discussion. 17 XXXI. "' Then my friend addressed me as follows: "This young girl whom you see, O stranger, was exposed in her earliest infancy; her mother, for reasons which you shall learn later, abandoned her to the mercy of Fortune. I found her and adopted her; for it was not permitted me to abandon without assistance a soul which had once formed part of a human body; this is one of the precepts of us Gymnosophists,1 whose lessons I have for some time been privileged to hear. Besides, it seemed to me that divine light beamed from the eyes of the child, which were fixed upon me with a keen and, at the same time, winning glance. With her was exposed a necklace of precious stones, which I showed you just now; and, upon a silken fillet, the story of the child was traced, in the language and characters of her country; it was no doubt her mother who, in her anxiety, had deposited with her these tokens whereby she might be recognised. What was written told me who she was and the name of her parents. I took her to a country house at some distance from the city, and gave her to my shepherds to bring up, with strict instructions to tell no one. I myself kept the 1 The naked philosophers of India. things which had been exposed with her, for fear they might lead to attempts upon her life. Thus, at the commencement, she lived in concealment; but, in the course of time, as she grew up, and increased in stature and beauty—to such an extent that, even if she had been hidden beneath the earth, her charms could not long have remained concealed—being afraid that the secret of her life might become noised abroad, and that, if any misfortune happened to her, the result would be disastrous for myself, I contrived to secure the appointment of ambassador to the satrap of Egypt. When I came here, I brought the girl with me, in order to make all necessary arrangements for her safety. I shall soon discuss my mission with the satrap, who has given me an audience for to-day. Meanwhile, I intrust this young girl to your care and that of the gods who have thus decided; I place her in your hands on the conditions agreed upon between us; namely, that you will always keep her free as you have received her from my hands, or rather, from the hands of the mother who exposed her; and that you will never marry her to anyone but a free man. I believe that you will faithfully carry out our agreement; I put my faith, not only in your oath, but also in your character, which I have carefully studied during the time that you have been in the city, and which I see is truly that of a Greek. XXXII. "'To-day I ought to have limited myself to this rapid outline, for the affairs of my embassy claim my attention; but if you will meet me at the temple of Isis to-morrow, I will give you full and accurate details concerning the young girl."

"' According to his wishes, I took the young girl, closely veiled, to my house. I spent the day in lavishing affection and caresses upon her; I offered thanks to God; already I looked upon her as a daughter, and called her such. The following morning, at daybreak, I hurried eagerly to the temple of Isis, where I had arranged to meet the stranger. I walked about for some time, waiting for him; and at length, seeing nothing of him, I went to the satrap's palace and asked whether anyone had seen the Aethiopian ambassador. They told me that he had left, or rather, had been driven out of the city, the satrap having threatened to put him to death if he had not crossed the frontiers by sunset. When I asked the reason, I was told that his mission had been to forbid the satrap from working the emerald mines, which he claimed as the property of Aethiopia. I went away deeply grieved, as if someone had dealt me a violent blow; I was also greatly disappointed at being thus prevented from learning who the young girl was, and the name of her native country and her parents.'" "Do not feel surprised," said Cnemon; "I myself am greatly vexed at not hearing; but perhaps I shall know later." "You shall," said Calasiris; "in the meantime, I will continue Charicles's story.

XXXIII. "'When I reached my house, the child came out to meet me. She could not talk to me, since she did not know him; and at length, seeing nothing of him, I went to the satrap's palace and asked whether anyone had seen the Aethiopian ambassador. They told me that he had left, or rather, had been driven out of the city, the satrap having threatened to put him to death if he had not crossed the frontiers by sunset. When I asked the reason, I was told that his mission had been to forbid the satrap from working the emerald mines, which he claimed as the property of Aethiopia. I went away deeply grieved, as if someone had dealt me a violent blow; I was also greatly disappointed at being thus prevented from learning who the young girl was, and the name of her native country and her parents.'" "Do not feel surprised," said Cnemon; "I myself am greatly vexed at not hearing; but perhaps I shall know later." "You shall," said Calasiris; "in the meantime, I will continue Charicles's story. XXXIII. " When I reached my house, the child came out to meeJH,e could not talk to me, since know Greek; but she took my hand by way of welcome, and the sight of her cheered my soul. I beheld with astonishment how, like young dogs of good breed which fawn even upon those of whom they have but little knowledge, she had from the very first understood my kindly feelings towards her, and regarded me as her father. I resolved not to stop at Catadupi, for fear some envious spirit might rob me of my second daughter. I accordingly went down the Nile until I reached the sea, where I found a ship to take me back to my native land. The child is now with me; she is my daughter, she bears my name; she is my only support. She has in every respect surpassed my wishes, when I consider how rapidly she has learnt Greek,

and her beauty has reached perfection, like a thriving plant. She so surpasses all other girls in beauty, that she attracts the admiration of all, both Greeks and strangers. Wherever she appears, in the temples, in the walks, in the public places, like a perfectly-finished statue, she draws upon herself the eyes and attention of all.

And yet, in spite of all these perfections, she causes me incurable sorrow; she rejects all ideas of marriage, and declares that she will remain a maiden all her life; devoting herself entirely to the service of Diana,1 she does nothing but hunt and shoot, while my life has become an unbearable burden. I had hoped to marry her to my nephew, an agreeable young man, distinguished by his character and abilities; but her cruel decision has frustrated my desires. Neither attention, nor exhortation, nor argument can persuade her. The most cruel thing of all is, that she turns my own weapons against me. The varied learning with which I have filled her mind is employed by her to prove that the mode of life which she has adopted is the best; she praises virginity to the skies, shows it seated by the side of the immortal gods, calls it pure, free from reproach, and uncorrupted, while she rejects with horror the idea of Love, Venus, and all the pomp and ceremonial of marriage. For this reason I appeal to you for assistance; it is for this reason that I have seized the 1 As a faKopos, or attendant, in her temple.

opportunity chance has given me to tell you this story, which I have been unable to make shorter. Wherefore, good Calasiris, grant me this favour: employ against her all the wisdom and enchantments of Egypt; lead her, by word and deed, to the feelings of her sex; make her understand that she is a woman. This will be easy enough for you, if you will; she is by no means averse to talking with men, she has been brought up in their company from her earliest childhood; she lives very close to you, in the sacred precincts of the temple. Do not refuse my prayer; do not let me drag out a melancholy old age, without children, without consolation, without heirs; I entreat you by Apollo himself and the gods of your country.' I shed tears at this story, my dear Cnemon; he himself mingled tears with his supplications; I promised to assist him in any way I could. XXXIV. "We were still deliberating, when a messenger arrived in haste to announce that the chief of the sacred embassy of the Aenianians had been at the door for some time, and was impatiently asking for the priest to begin the religious ceremonies. I asked Charicles who the Aenianians were, what was the nature of their embassy, and what sacrifice they were going to offer. 'The Aenianians,' he replied,'are the chief people of Thessaly; they are a genuine Hellenic people, since they are the descendants of Hellen, the son of Deucalion. They dwell on the shores of the Malian gulf, and pride themselves on having Hypata for their metropolis; this city is so named, according to them, because it commands1 the other cities of the province and rules over them, or, as others declare, because it is built at the foot of Mount Oeta. As for the sacrifice and the sacred embassy, the Aenianians despatch one every four years in honour of Neoptolemus, son of Achilles, at the time of the celebration of the Pythian games, which, as you know, are now going on. For it was here, at the foot of the altar of Apollo, that Neoptolemus was treacherously slain by Orestes, son of Agamemnon. The present embassy surpasses all preceding ones in magnificence: for the head of itboasts that he is descended from Achilles. I met him yesterday, and he appeared worthy to be a member of the house-of Peleus; his beauty, his lofty stature, clearly show him to be descended from a goddess.' 1 'Yira-rtvei. 2 'ytt Oitq. 18—2

"I asked with surprise how he, being an Aenianian, could claim to be a descendant of Achilles, since the Egyptian Homer, in his poems, makes Achilles a native of Phthia. Charicles replied: 'In this the young man, in common with the rest of the Aenianians, claims Achilles as his countryman; he declares that Thetis, when she left the Malian gulf, married Peleus, and that the countries washed by this gulf formerly bore the name of Phthia; that others, allured by the reputation of Achilles, have falsely claimed the honour of having given him birth. He is also descended from Achilles in another way: he reckons amongst his ancestors Mnestheus, the son of Sperchius and Polydora, daughter of Peleus, one of the most famous of Achilles' companions at Troy, who, from his close connection with him, was chief of the commanders of the Myrmidons. Lastly, in order to complete his connection with Achilles, whom he claims in a manner as the property of the Aenianians, he appeals, amongst other proofs, to the offering sent to Neoptolemus, an offering which the Thessalians have agreed to» leave to the Aenianians, thereby admitting that they are more closely related to him.' 'I do not grudge them that,' said I, 'whether the statement be really true, or due to selfglorification; but call in the ambassador; for I am exceedingly anxious to see him.' XXXV. "Charicles consented, and the young man came in. There was really something about him that reminded me of Achilles; his proud looks, his head erect, his hair carelessly thrown back over his forehead; his nose revealed an impetuous disposition; his open nostrils freely inhaled the air; his dark blue eyes were at the same time proud and gentle, like the surface of the sea when a storm is succeeded by a calm. He saluted us in the usual way, and we returned his salute. He then told us that the time was come to offer sacrifice to the god, in order that he might afterwards have time to accomplish the expiatory sacrifice in honour of the god and to arrange the funeral procession. 'So be it,' said Chancles, getting up. 'You will see Chariclea to-day,' he added to me, 'if you do not already know her; for, according to custom, she will take part in the procession and the funeral ceremonies in honour of Neoptolemus.' I knew the young girl, my dear Cnemon, and had frequently seen her, both when we were taking part in the same sacrifices, and when she came to put some question to me concerning sacred subjects. However, I made no an-

swer, being eager to see what was going to take place next. We immediately directed our steps towards the temple, where the Thessalians had already made all preparations for the sacrifice. When we had reached the altar, the young man commenced the sacred ceremonies, after the priest had uttered a prayer. Then the Pythian goddess, from her inmost shrine, gave forth this oracle: 'Sing, O Delphi, of her who begins with grace and ends with glory1; sing of the 1 Xapi/cAeLa, from X"Pts and KaÉos. son of a goddess; when they leave my shrine, they shall cleave the waves, and arrive at the countries darkened by the heat of the sun. There they shall receive the noble meed of a virtuous life, a snowy crown on their dusky brows.' XXXVI. "At this declaration of the God, those who stood by were greatly perplexed, and asked one another what might be the meaning of the oracle; each interpreted the words in his own way and explained them in a manner that accorded with his inclinations. No one, however, saw their true purport; for oracles, like dreams, can only be judged after the event. Besides, the inhabitants of Delphi, struck with admiration, and eager to see the sacred procession, which was on a magnificent scale, did not trouble about exactly understanding the meaning of the oracle.

END Of Book и BOOK III

I. "When the ceremony was over, and the procession had gone by "continued Calasiris. "But," interrupted Cnemon, "it is not yet over for me; your narrative has not yet made me a spectator of it: when I am burning with anxiety to hear the whole story, and to be a spectator ot the ceremony myself, you pass me by and treat me like one who has come, in the words of the proverb, too late for the feast; as soon as you have opened the theatre, you shut the doors again." "I did not want to weary you with such details, which have nothing to do with our subject; I was in a hurry to reach the principal part of my narrative, about which you asked me at the commencement; but, since you wish to be a passing spectator of the solemnity (just like an Athenian), I will give you a brief description of the pageant, one of the few that has become celebrated, both on its own account and because of the results which followed it.

"At the head of the procession was a hecatomb of victims, led by some of the initiated, men of rustic dress and appearance. Each of them was clad in a white tunic, tied round the waist. The right arm, bare to the shoulder and the breast, brandished a two-edged axe. The oxen, completely black, walked along majestically; their necks were proudly arched; on their foreheads were horns exactly alike, scarcely bent, some gilded, and others adorned with flowers; their feet were broad and short, their dewlaps deep and hanging down as far as the knees. A hundred in number, they formed a true hecatomb. They were followed by a number of victims of different kinds, each walking separately and in order. They proceeded to the accompaniment of flutes and pipes, playing a mystic strain, that heralded the sacrifice.

II. "After the animals and their drivers came some young Thessalian girls, with beautiful and deep girdles and flowing hair. They formed two bands; the first carried baskets of flowers and fruits; the second, vessels full of cakes and perfumes which scented the air around. These offerings, being carried on their heads, did not prevent them from using their hands. Arranged in long rows, some straight, the others slanting, holding each other by the hand, they advanced and joined in the dance. The first company gave the keynote of the song; its only duty was to sing the sacred hymn, the subject of which was the praises of Peleus and Thetis, then of their son, and then of Neopto lemus. After them, my dear Cnemon"

"No more 'dear Cnemons'; you are cheating me again of a very great pleasure, in not letting me hear the words of the hymn; it seems that you want to make me a mere spectator of the ceremony, instead of an auditor." "Very well, then," replied Calasiris, "if you so desire it, you shall hear; as far as I remember, the words of the hymn were nearly as follows: 'I sing of Thetis, Thetis with the golden hair, immortal daughter of Nereus of the sea, wedded to Peleus by the will of Jupiter, glory of the seas, our Venus of Paphos. She it was who bore the mighty, the hero of battle, the divine Achilles, whose glory reaches the heavens. The son of Achilles and Pyrrha was Neoptolemus, who destroyed the city of Troy and defended the Greeks. Be thou propitious to us, O hero, son of Achilles, blessed Neoptolemus, who here reposest in the territory sacred to Apollo; receive this sacrifice favourably and drive away fear from our city. I sing of Thetis, Thetis with the golden hair.' III. "Such, my dear Cnemon, if my memory does not deceive me, were the words of the hymn. In the dances there was such grace and regularity, every movement was so happily wedded to the melody of the song, that for a while the spectators forgot to look, being entirely abandoned to the pleasure of listening, and all who were looking on followed the young girls as they passed in front of them, irresistibly carried away by the delightful harmony. But, when a band of youths on horseback appeared behind, with a splendidly-attired commander, the magnificent spectacle soon effaced the pleasure of listening. They were only fifty in all, divided into two bodies of five-and-twenty; in their midst was the chief of the sacred embassy under their protection. Their greaves, plaited with purple leather thongs, were tied above the ankle; their white cloaks, with purple borders round the bottom, were fastened with golden clasps over their breasts. All their horses were Thessalian and recalled in their fiery looks the freedom of their native plains; they champed their bits and covered them with foam, as if scorning a master, but nevertheless obeyed the guiding hand of their riders, in whichever direction they turned them; they were adorned with trappings and frontlets, gorgeously bedecked with silver and gold, so curiously wrought that it seemed as if the youths had vied with one another in their efforts.

"But, in spite of the brilliancy and magnificence of this procession, the

eyes of the spectators passed it by in contempt, and fixed themselves upon the commander, my charge Theagenes, who seemed to eclipse all who had hitherto appeared, as a bright lightning flash eclipses the lesser fires of heaven, so brilliant was the show he made. Horseman and foot-soldier at once, heavily armed, he brandished an ashen spear with a point of brass, his beaver up, with face exposed, clad in a cloak of purple, upon which was embroidered in gold the combat between the Lapithae and Centaurs; on the amber buckle that fastened it was represented the image of Pallas, holding before her the Gorgon's head on her shield. A gentle breeze added to his charms; sweetly breathing, it softly played with the curls upon his neck, parted his hair upon his forehead, and made the borders of his robe float over his charger's back and legs. It seemed, to look at his neck arched like the waves, his head erect, his pricked-up ears, and his fiery, swiftly glancing eyes, as if the animal himself were conscious of his master's beauty, and, proud of his noble form, felt that he carried the noblest rider of all. Proud of the burden which he bore and of the hand which guided him, he moved along freely with reins loosely held, balancing himself alternately on either side, lightly skimming the surface of the ground with the extremity of his hoofs, rocking his rider by a regular and gentle motion. All gazed with admiration upon the sight; the masculine features and beauty of the young man conquered all hearts. The women, unable to disguise their feelings, flung him fruits and flowers, in the hope of obtaining a favour from him; in short, all were agreed that Theagenes was the handsomest man who had ever been seen.

IV. "But, when rosy-fingered morn appeared (to use the words of Homer), when the beautiful and accomplished Chariclea left the temple of Diana, then we saw that even Theagenes might be surpassed, but only in the sense that the most perfect beauty is always less graceful and attractive in men than in women. She rode in a chariot drawn by two per fectly white oxen; a purple cloak, embroidered with gold, enveloped her down to her feet. Round her waist was a girdle, a masterpiece of work, the like of which never had been, and never would be seen. It represented two serpents, the tails of which were intertwined over her back; their necks, brought beneath her bosom, formed by their interlacing a graceful knot, from the midst of which their heads hung down on one side and the other as an appendage; you would have said that the serpents not only appeared to climb, but really did so; so life-like were they. Their aspect was neither frightful nor alarming; they rather seemed to be buried in a languid sleep and lulled by the pleasure of reposing upon the young girl's bosom. They were wrought in dark-coloured gold, which had been artificially blackened, in order to represent, by this mixture of black and gold colour, the roughness and changing appearance of the scales. Such was the maiden's girdle. Her hair was not completely tressed up, nor quite unconfined; the greater part of it, flowing down her neck, waved luxuriantly over her back and shoulders; tender branches of laurel, intertwined with the locks on her forehead and crown, formed a kind of garland, in which the freshness of the rose mingled with the dazzling reflection of the sun, and prevented her tresses from floating too freely in the breeze. In her left hand she held a bow; a quiver hung over her right shoulder; in her right hand she carried a lighted torch, the brightness of which paled before the brilliancy of her eyes." "It is certainly they, Theagenes and Chariclea," cried Cnemon. "And where are they? Show them to me, in Heaven's name, I implore you," said Calasiris, believing that Cnemon saw them at that moment. "My father," replied Cnemon, "I only thought that I saw them, although in their absence; so faithfully have you described them as I knew them." "I do not know," continued Calasiris, "whether you have seen them such as Greece and the sun beheld them on that day, in all their splendour, amidst universal applause—she the object of all men's, he of all women's desires; for there was no one who would not have considered it immortality to be united to one or the other. But, while the inhabitants more particularly admired the young man, the Thessalians favoured the maiden, each being most struck with the one whom he saw for the first time. For that which is novel strikes the eyes with greater effect than that with which we are familiar. But, what a sweet illusion, what a delightful anticipation! how you made my heart flutter with hope, when I thought that you saw, and intended to show me those beloved children! And now it seems that you have completely deceived me! You assured me, at the commencement of our conversation, that they would be here directly; it was for this that you demanded my story as a reward; already evening and night are come upon us, and they are not here; you are unable to show them to me." "Do not be uneasy," he replied, "be of good cheer, they will certainly come; no doubt something has detained them and prevented them from arriving as soon as we had agreed. Besides, even if I have not yet shown them to you, neither have I received my reward in full; if, then, you are in a hurry to see them, carry out your promise and finish your story. " "I rather shrink from the last part of it," said Calasiris, "both on my own account, by reason of the melancholy recollections which it awakens, and also on yours, because I am afraid of wearying you by my interminable story. But, since you seem a patient listener, and eager to hear stories that are worth telling, I will resume my narrative at the place where I left off. But first let us light a lamp, and offer the evening libations to the gods of night,1 in order that, having performed this sacred duty, we may continue our narrative with perfect safety through the night." keep away from him unpleasant dreams, and to let him see, at least in sleep, those whom he so dearly loved. After this, he continued his story as follows: "After the procession had compassed the tomb of Neoptolemus and the young men had thrice ridden round it, the women uttered mournful cries, and the men raised warlike shouts. Immediately, as at a giv-

en signal, oxen, rams and goats were slaughtered; it seemed as if they had all been put to death by a single hand. An enormous altar was covered with a heap of fragments of wood, and, after the consecrated portions of the victims had been placed on the top, they begged the priest of Apollo to begin the libations and set light to the fire beneath the altar. Charicles replied that it was really his duty to pour the libations; but that the chief of the sacred embassy ought to light the fire with the torch which the priestess should hand to him, according to custom. With these words, he poured the libation, and Theagenes received the torch from Chariclea. Then, my dear Cnemon, what took

V. With these words, the old man gave orders to a servant, who brought a lighted lamp; and he immediately proceeded to pour libations, to invoke the gods, and, before all, Mercury, whom he begged to 1 *Literally,* "take the last cup before going to bed." 20 place convinced us that there is in our souls something divine, and that they are in a manner allied to some higher nature. For, as soon as they beheld each other, they loved; it seemed as if their souls had recognised that they were akin, as if, conscious that they were related by nobility, they hastened with a bound each towards its affinity.

"At first they remained dumbfounded and motionless; she, still holding out the torch, and he, extending his hand to take it. For a long time they continued thus, their eyes fixed upon each other, as if, instead of having now met for the first time, they had met before, and were trying to remember where. Then they smiled, gently and almost imperceptibly, which was only betrayed by the movement of their eyes; soon, as if ashamed, they both blushed; and, a moment later, when passion had reached their hearts, they grew pale. In a word, a thousand changes overspread their faces in a moment, a thousand changes of colour and features betrayed the agitation of their soul. All this, as may be imagined, escaped the notice of the multitude, whose thoughts and attention were devoted to other matters. Charicles himself, busy in reciting the customary prayer and invocation, saw nothing of it either; but as for me, my whole attention was devoted to watching the young people; for, after I had heard the oracle that had been given to Theagenes, at the time when he was offering sacrifice in the temple, their names awakened in me some suspicion of what was going to happen, although I could not clearly make out the meaning of that part of the prophecy that related to the future.

VI. "At last, Theagenes tore himself away from the maiden, as if under compulsion, placed the torch beneath the altar, and lighted the pile. The procession broke up¡ the Thessalians repaired to a banquet, and the rest dispersed to their own houses. Chariclea threw a white robe over her shoulders, and retired with some of her companions to her abode in the precincts of the temple; for she did not live with her supposed father, but apart, in order that she might devote herself entirely to the service of the temple. Filled with curiosity by what I had seen and heard, I purposely went to meet Charicles. 'Well,' said he, 'have you seen Char idea, my pride and the pride of Delphi?' 'Yes, and not for the first time,' I replied; 'I had already frequently met her before in the temple; not merely in passing by, as the phrase goes; she has frequently offered sacrifice with me; she has often questioned me concerning things human and divine, when she came across anything that puzzled her, and I was pleased to assist her.' 'And what did you think of her to-day? Did she add any ornament to the procession?' 'Hush, Charicles; you might as well ask me whether the moon outshines the stars.' 'But some praise was given to the Thessalian youth.' 'Yes, to him was given the second or third place, but all were agreed that your daughter was the pride and crown of the procession.' Charicles was evidently pleased at my words, and, while I told the truth, I attained my object, which was to inspire him with perfect confidence in me. He smiled and said to me: 'I am now going to her; if you would like it, do not hesitate to come with me and see whether the crowd and the disturbance have fatigued her.' I gladly consented, giving him to understand that I had nothing more at heart than the wish to oblige him. VII. "When we reached her room, we found her lying on her couch, in a state of languor and depression, her eyes moist with the tears of love. Her father, having embraced her as usual, asked her what ailed her. She complained of a violent headache, and said that she would like to rest. Then Charicles left the room with me, ordered the servants to keep quiet, and, going out into the front of the house, said: 'What does this mean, my dear Calasiris? What is this languor which has come over my daughter?' 'Do not be surprised,' I replied, 'if, while walking in procession amidst so large a crowd, she has drawn upon her some evil eye.' At these words he smiled ironically: 'And do you also, like the vulgar, believe in the influence of the evil eye?' 'I be lieve in it implicitly, and the following is my explanation of the matter. The air which surrounds us and penetrates into our bodies through the eyes, nose, respiration, and other passages, reaches us charged with external qualities, and, according to the different nature of these qualities, we are variously affected. After that, it is enough for anyone to look at a beautiful object with an envious eye to communicate pernicious qualities to the surrounding air; his breath spreads, full of bitterness, over his neighbour, and, thanks to its subtilty, penetrates to the bones, even to the very marrow. Thus it is that, frequently, this species of envy which has been called by the name of "fascination," affects the health of those whom it attacks. To convince you of this, Charicles, I would ask you to remember that we are frequently attacked by ophthalmia or some contagious disease, without having touched persons afflicted by them, without having been near their bed or sat at the same table with them, but simply because we have breathed the same air. Remember again—and there is not a more evident proof—the manner of the birth of love; objects perceived by the sight produce

it; they spread around themselves a kind of light mist, and cause the passion, which is to have its abode in the soul, to penetrate through the channel of the eyes. And it is not difficult to see the reason of this: the sight, being the most fiery and mobile of all our senses, is for that very reason most susceptible to the influences around it; and, by reason of its burning spirit, attracts the emanations of love. VIII. " But, if you wish for an example out of natural history, I will give you one out of the sacred books on animals: the Charadrius1 possesses the property of curing the jaundice; when anyone afflicted with this complaint looks at it, it turns aside, shuts its eyes, and runs away; not, as is sometimes said, because it is unwilling to bestow its assistance, but because, from the moment that an afflicted person looks upon it, it naturally attracts, as it were, a 1 Supposed to be the "stone-curlew"; so called from dwelling in "clefts" *(x-Pafyal)* current of the disease; for this reason it avoids the person's eyes, like a dart. It is the same with the serpent called basilisk1; you have no doubt heard that its breath and look alone dry up and infect everything that it touches. Nor must we be astonished if some persons fascinate even their dearest friends, those to whom they wish every happiness; for, being naturally envious, they do not do what they wish, but what their nature compels them to do.' IX. "After a moment's silence, Chancles rejoined: 'You have solved the question in a reasonable and convincing manner; pray Heaven that the fascination which influences her may be that of love; far from considering that a malady, I should think that she was cured. You know that I have already begged your assistance in this. But, for the moment, there seems no reason to suspect this; she is the declared enemy of love and marriage. We must therefore believe that her malady is really due to the evil eye. I do not doubt that you will consent to cure her of it; for you are my friend, and your 1 Perhaps the Cobra Capello. 21 learning is vast.' I promised that I would do all that fay in my power to help her, if I found that there was anything the matter with her.

X. "We were still discussing the matter, when a messenger arrived in great haste: 'My good friends,' said he, 'one would think you were invited to a fray instead of a feast, you are so slow in coming. Have you forgotten that it is the handsome Theagenes who has prepared it, and that the greatest of heroes, Neoptolemus, presides at it? Come, then; do not make us wait until evening; we are only waiting for you.' Charicles whispered to me: 'This man's invitation is somewhat rude1; he shows no signs of the good manners of Bacchus, although he has imbibed pretty freely. But, let us go, for I am afraid that he may in the end proceed to violence.' 'You are joking,' I said; 'however, let us go.' As soon as we had arrived, Theagenes placed Charicles next to himself, and also treated me with 1 *Literally,* "he has brought the invitation of the stick." respect for his sake. But why need I weary you with lengthy details of the feast, the dances of maidens, the music, the Pyrrhic dance of the youths in armour, and other entertainments with which Theagenes graced his magnificent banquet, and the exquisite dishes which rendered the repast more agreeable and conduced to conviviality? I will, however, tell you things which it is necessary you should know, and which will give me pleasure to relate. Theagenes assumed a look of cheerfulness, and forced himself to entertain the company, but I saw in what direction his thoughts were tending. He kept rolling his eyes; from time to time he heaved a deep sigh without any apparent reason; at one time dejected and deep in thought, he suddenly became more cheerful, as if he were conscious of his manner and wished to recover himself; in short, he passed rapidly from one extreme to the other. The mind of a lover, like that of a drunken man, is changeable and inconstant; both seem to be tossed upon the waves of passion; wherefore a lover is prone to intoxication, and a drunken man to love.

XI. "At last, when he appeared overcome by languor and ill at ease, all the guests were convinced that he was unwell. Then Charicles, who had observed nothing but his changes of humour, whispered to me: 'Some evil eye has also looked upon him; he seems to me in the same state as Chariclea.' 'The very same, by Isis!' I replied; 'and not without reason; for, next after her, he was the most observed in all the procession.' When the time came for the cup to be handed round, Theagenes, although against his will, drank first to the health of all his guests. When it came to me, I thanked him for the compliment, but said I would not drink; whereupon he darted at me a look of rage, considering himself slighted. Charicles, perceiving this, said: 'This man drinks no wine and does not eat the flesh of any creature that has lived.' When Theagenes enquired the reason of this, he said: 'He is an Egyptian from Memphis, and a priest of Isis.' When Theagenes heard these words, he was suddenly filled with a great joy, and, rising upright, like one who has lighted upon a treasure, he asked for water, and, having pledged me, said: 'O wisest of men, at least take this cup from me; it contains the liquor that you love best, and let this table conclude a league of friendship between us.' 'So be it, noble Theagenes,' I answered; 'I have long been well disposed towards you.' With these words, I took the cup and drank.

"Then the banquet came to an end, and each of us prepared to retire; I also withdrew, after Theagenes had taken a warmer farewell of me than our existing acquaintance justified. When I reached my lodging, I could not sleep; I could think of nothing but Theagenes and Chariclea and the meaning of the last part of the oracle. When it was midnight, I thought I saw Apollo and Diana (if indeed I did not really see them). They handed over to me Theagenes and Chariclea, and, addressing me by name, said: 'It is time for you to return to your native land; such is the decree of Fate. Leave this country; take with you these two young people; treat them as your children, and lead them out of the land of Egypt, where and how the gods shall please.' XII. "Having thus spoken, they

disappeared, leaving me convinced. that it was not a vision, but a reality. I did not doubt that what I had seen was a reality, but I did not know to what country or people I was to lead them." "This you will be able to tell me afterwards," said Cnemon; "but how can you assert that the gods really appeared to you in person, and that it was not a dream?" "In the same manner as Homer the sage tells us in a riddle, which has passed unheeded by many. He says somewhere: 'I recognised the traces of his feet and legs, as he departed; the Gods are easily known.'" "I confess," said Cnemon, "that I myself am one of the many; perhaps you have only quoted this passage to convince me; I have never attached any deeper meaning to it than the ordinary one, which I found in it when I heard it for the first time; I did not know what theological principles were contained in it." XIII. After a few moments' silence and reflection, during which he seemed to be meditating upon some holy mystery, Calasiris went on to say: "The gods and spirits come to us and leave us most frequently in human form, rarely in the shape of other animals, that they may be known to our fancy in the likeness of ourselves. Although the profane do not recognise them, they cannot escape the eyes of the wise; they may be easily distinguished by their fixed eyes and eyelids, which never move, but even more readily by their walk, which does not consist, like ours, in the alternate movement of the feet; they seem to glide and fly rapidly through the air, which they cleave rather than traverse. For this reason, the Egyptian statues of the gods have the feet joined; Homer, being an Egyptian and skilled in sacred lore, also knew this, and expressed it symbolically, leaving it for those to understand him who were able. Thus, of Pallas he says, 'her terrible eyes flashed fire'; of Neptune, 'I recognised the traces of his feet and legs, as he departed,' where the word *pel* refers to his 'flowing motion,' and does not mean 'easily,' as some have wrongly interpreted it." XIV. "O most divine Calasiris," said Cnemon, "you have initiated me into a holy mystery. But I notice that you have two or three times called Homer an Egyptian, which perhaps no one has ever heard; I do not indeed disbelieve it, but, as your statement greatly surprises me, I beg you will not leave it unexplained." "Although it is foreign to my subject, I will endeavour to satisfy you in a few words. I am quite willing that other countries should claim the honour of being the birthplace of Homer; the wise man's country is the world; but he was in fact an Egyptian, born at 'hundredgated Thebes,' as he himself calls it; his father was Mercury, although commonly supposed to be one of the priests of that god. The truth is that, when the wife of this priest, having performed certain purificatory rites, went to sleep in the temple, the god lay with her and begat Homer, who at his birth bore traces of his illegitimate origin. When he came into the world, one of his thighs was covered with long hair. He was called Homer, because he wandered from one country to another, chiefly in Greece, singing his poems. He himself did not mention his own name, nor that of his native place, nor of his family; but those who knew of the mark on his body, gave him this name. "1 "But why, my father, did he say nothing about his native country?" "Perhaps he was ashamed of having been driven from it; for he had been banished by his father, when he presented himself for initiation on arriving at man's estate, because the mark on his body betrayed his bastard origin; or perhaps he in his shrewdness refrained from giving the name, so that, by concealing it, he might claim every city in the world as his birthplace."sublimity and charm of Egypt, and are transcendent in style, they would assuredly never have so excelled all others, had they not been built upon a divine foundation." But, after you had detected the gods according to the indications given by Homer, tell me what you did next." "I remained awake as before, reflecting amid the silence of the night, so favourable to meditation. I rejoiced that I had succeeded beyond my hopes, and at the thought that I should soon return to my country; but I was deeply grieved at the idea that Charicles would be deprived of his daughter. I did not know how I should take the young people away and prepare them for their departure. I was at a loss how I was to keep our flight a secret and which way I should direct my course; whether we should travel by land or sea; I was tossed by a storm of anxious thoughts, and could not close my eyes. XV. "What you say seems probable," said Cnemon. "When I think of his poems, which contain a mixture of the l Apparently deriving it from *prlpbs,* a thigh. XVI. "It was hardly daylight, when I heard a knocking at the door of the hall, and the voice of a young man calling.

When my servant asked who it was that knocked and what he wanted, he replied: 'Say that it is Theagenes the Thessalian.' I was delighted when I heard that it was the young man, and ordered him to be admitted, thinking that Fortune herself offered me the opportunity of carrying out my plans. I thought that, having learnt during the banquet that I was an Egyptian and a priest, he had come to ask my assistance in his love-affair, being, I imagine, of the same opinion of the majority of mankind, who erroneously believe that all Egyptians are equally learned. There is one kind of knowledge which is vulgar, and, so to speak, crawls upon the ground, the handmaid of idols ever busied with dead bodies, engrossed in the study of herbs and devoted to incantations, as useless to itself as to those who consult it, and in many ways self-contradictory; its successes are mean and sordid, chimeras in place of realities and frustrated hopes; in short, it is the inventor of abominable practices and the minister of infamous pleasures. The other kind, my son, which is truly wisdom, of which the former is the bastard daughter, is practised by us priests and ministers of religion from our earliest days. It lifts its gaze aloft to heavenly things, holds converse with the gods, and participates in the higher nature, investigating the movements of the heavenly bodies, and thence acquiring a knowledge of the future; far removed from all the

ills which afflict humanity, it studies to arrange everything with a view to what is good and profitable for mankind. It was this wisdom that exiled me from my country for a time, to avoid, if possible, the evils which it foretold to me and the fratricidal quarrel of my sons. But let the Gods and the Fates decide; the issue rests with them. It was not so much, I believe, in order to spare my eyes this dreadful sight, as to make me discover Chariclea, that they have banished me from my native land, as you will learn from the sequel.

XVII. "When Theagenes had entered my room, after mutual salutations, I made him sit down upon my bed, and asked him what pressing business had brought him to me so early. Having passed his hand several times over his face, he replied: 'My happiness is at stake, but I am ashamed to tell you the reason,' and then he was silent. I perceived that it was time for me to act the wizard, and to pretend to divine what I already knew. I looked at him kindly and said: 'Although you are afraid to speak, nothing can be concealed from the Gods and our wisdom.' Then, after a few moments' silence, arranging some little pebbles in my hand, as if counting, although I had nothing to count, I shook my locks, like those possessed by prophetic frenzy, and said: 'My son, you are in love.' At these prophetic words, he started; and, when I added the name of Chariclea, thinking that my knowledge was divinely inspired, he was ready to throw himself at my feet and worship me. When I restrained him, he embraced me several times, and thanked Heaven that he had not been deceived in his hopes, and entreated me to save him, declaring that he could not live without speedy assistance; that the violence of XVIII. "While he thus entreated me and promised me his whole fortune as a reward, a messenger came from Charicles. 'Charicles begs you will go to him,' said he; 'he is here, hard by, in the temple of Apollo, where he is chanting a hymn to appease the god, having been alarmed by a dream.' I immediately got up, dismissed Theagenes, and hurried to the temple, where I found Charicles sitting in a chair, overwhelmed with grief, and sighing. I went up to him and asked him why he was so gloomy and sorrowful. He replied: 'How could I be otherwise? I have had a fearful dream; and I have heard that my daughter is ill, and that she has not closed her eyes all night. Her sickness is the more grievous to me, since to-morrow is the day on which the priestess of Diana, in accordance with the laws, ought to present a torch to the armed runners and bestow upon them the prize of victory. Thus, one of two things must happen; either Chariclea will violate established custom by absenting herself, or, if she takes part in the ceremony against his affliction and the ardour of the passion by which his heart, which had never felt the fire of love, was consumed, required prompt treatment. He swore that he had never known a woman, that he had always spurned them and despised the idea of love and marriage, until Chariclea's beauty had proved to him that he was naturally weak, but that he had never until then beheld a woman worthy of his love. At the same time he shed tears, to show that he had been overcome by a woman against his will. I tried to comfort and console him, saying: 'Do not despair, since you have had recourse to me; she will not be able to prevail against my wisdom. It is true that her morals are austere, and that it may be a hard task to bring her to love, since she hates even the very name of Venus and marriage; but for your sake I will do all I can; art can conquer nature; only do not lose courage, and be ready to obey my commands implicitly.' He promised to follow my instructions, even though I should bid him walk over naked swords. her wish, she will aggravate her malady. Wherefore, even if it could not be done before, assist her and apply some remedy; justice, friendship, and the respect due to the gods demand this from you. I know that it is easy for you, as you say yourself, to cure the charm of an evil eye, if you will; nothing is too difficult for the priests of your country to perform.' I confessed that I had been somewhat remiss, in order to mislead him, and asked him to give me a day to prepare some medicine for her. 'For the present,' I said, 'let us go and see your daughter, examine her condition, and comfort her » as best we can. At the same time, I wish you would say something about me to the girl, and make her better acquainted with me; so that, becoming more familiar, she may have greater confidence in my power to cure her.' 'Be it so,' he replied; 'let us go.'

XIX. "I need not describe the condition in which we found Chariclea. Her affliction had overwhelmed her; the roses had faded from her cheeks, and the fire of her eyes had been quenched by the constant flow of tears. However, when she saw us, she composed herself, and endeavoured to assume her ordinary voice and expression. Charicles, having kissed and fondled her, said: 'O my daughter, will you not tell your father what ails you? Now that an evil eye has fascinated you, do you keep silence, as if you had done wrong, and had not received an injury from the eyes that have looked upon you so balefully? But, be of good cheer. I have entreated the wise Calasiris to find some means of curing you; he can do so, for he excels all other men in divine knowledge, being a priest, and, what is more, our especial friend. Wherefore you will do well to receive him with confidence; put yourself in his hands, whether he wishes to employ incantations or any other means of healing you. Besides, you are not averse to the society of the learned.' Chariclea made no reply, but nodded her head, in token that she would be glad to listen to my advice. We then left her. Charicles reminded me of my promise that I would do my best to find a way to arouse in Chariclea an inclination to men and marriage. I gave him my word that his wish would soon be satisfied, and sent him on his way rejoicing. 7 lb. (S. Warschewiczki interpreted J. Bourde lotius emendavit, supplevit, ac libros decem animadversionum adjecit, Gr. et Lat. Apud P. L. Febvrier. Lutetiae Parisiorum, 1619, 8vo. 8 lb. Collatione MSS. Bibliothecae Palatinae et aliorum emendati et aucti cura D. Parei, Gr. et Lat. Francofurti, 1631.

9 C. W. Mitscherlich. Scriptores Erotici Graeci, 1792, 8vo. 10 G. A. Hirschig, 'EpioriKwv Aoyiov 2vyy pajtls: Erotici Scriptores Graeci. Paris (Didot), 1856.
11 Heliodori Aethiopicae historiae libri decern, nunc primum e Graeco sermone in Latinum translati, S. Warschewiczki interprete. Adjectum P. Melancthonis de ipso autore et hac ejusdem conversione judicium. Basileae, I552 12 Heliodorus, translated from the Greek by S.

Warschewiczki, Lugduni Batavorum, 1637.
13 Heliodori Aethiopicorum libri decern ab I.

Bekkero recogniti. Lipsiae, 1855. (Part of the Bibliotheca Scriptorum Graecorum et Romanorum Teubneriana.) 14 Martini Crush Aethiopicae Heliodori historiae epitome, cum observationibus ejusdem. Francofurti, 1584.
15 An Aethiopian Historie, written in Greek by

Heliodorus, no less wittie than pleasaunt. Englished by T. Underdowne, and newly corrected and augmented with divers and sundry additions by the said Authour. *Black Letter.* Imprinted for F. Coldocke. London, 1587, 4to.
16 lb. Printed for W. Cotton. London, 1606,4IO. 17 Another edition. Heliodorus, his Aethiopian

History, done out of Greeke by T. Underdowne and compared by the editor, W. Barret, with other translations in divers languages for W. Barret. London, 1622, 4to.
18 The beginning of Heliodorus, his Aethiopical

History in Hexameters. 1591, 4to.
19 The famous Historie of Heliodorus, amplified, augmented, and delivered paraphrastically in verse, by W. Lisle. London, 1638. 20 The Triumphs of Love and Constancy, a romance, containing the heroic amours of Theagenes and Chariclea. The first five books rendered by a person of quality, the last five by N. Tate. London, 1687. 21 The Adventures of Theagenes and Chariclea, 2 vols. London, 1717. 22 The Adventures of Theagenes and Chariclea, a romance translated from the Greek, 2 vols. London, 1789. 23 The Ethiopics, or Adventures of Theagenes and Chariclea, translated from the Greek, with notes by R. Smith. (Bonn's Classical Library.) 24 De Wonderlyke Liefde gefallen van Theagenes en Chariclea... In zuyver Nederduytsch overgebracht door J. Gentil, s' Gravenhaage, 1726. 25 M. v. Velden Calasires Sterfdagh. Ghenomen uyt de Historie van Heliodorus belaughende de kuysche Vryagie van Theagenes ende Chariclea (in 6 acts and in verse). Amstelredam, 1631. 26 L'Histoire Aethiopique de Heliodorus con tenant dix livres traitant des loyales et pudiques amours de Theagenes Thessalien et Chariclea Aethiopienne. Nouvellement traduite de Grec en Fran9ais by J. Amyot, Bishop of Auxerre. Paris, 1547, fol. £. Groulleau. 27 lb., fF. 296, Catherine Fontanel. Lyon, 1559. 28 lb., Lyon, 1559, 16mo. 29 lb., Paris, 1559, fol. 30 lb., Paris, ff» 320; 1560, 12010. 31 lb., Lyon, 1579, 16mo. 32 lb., Rouen, 1596, 16mo, T. Mallard. 33 An Aethiopian History written in Greek,

Englished by Thomas Underdowne, anno 1587, with introduction by Charles Whibley. The series of Tudor Translations, Vol. V., 1892.
34 Histoire Éthiopique d'Heliodore... traduc tion d'Amyot, revue et corrigée par M. Trognon, avec des notes de MM. Coray, etc., Paris, 1822. (Vol. II. of the Collection des Romanciers Grecs et Latins.) 35 Amours de Théagenes et Chariclée, traduction de J. Amyot, 1822. (Collection des Romans Grecs, Vols. II.-V.) 36 Les Adventures Amoureuse *sic* de Théagenes et Chariclée sommairement descrite (in verse) et representée par figures. Dedié Pierre Vallet, 1613, 4to. 37 Les chastes et loyales Amours de Théagène et
Chariclée, reduites du Grec de l'histoire d'Heliodore en huict poëmes dragmatiques ou théâtres consécutifs, par A. Hardy, Paris, 1623.
38 Les Amours de Théagène et Chariclée. His torie Éthiopique d'Heliodore. Traduction nouvelle (by J. de Montlyard). S. Thiboust, Paris, 1623. 39 Ib. Seconde édition, Paris, 1626. 40 Amours de Théagenes et Chariclée, historie
Éthiopique, translated from the Greek by
L. F. de Fontenu. Coustelier, Paris, 1743.
41 lb., 1782.
24 42 lb., Bibliotheque universelle des dames, 1785:

Romans, torn. 1-3.
43 Les Ethiopiennes d'Heliodore, ou, Theagene et Charicle-e, traduction de Quenneville, revue par L. Humbert, 1880. 44 Theagene et Charicle-e, translated by C. Zevort, 1856. 45 Heliodorus, oder eine sehr schone liebliche nutzliche Historie von Theagene und Chariclia, erstlichgriechisch beschriben nachmahlen in Latin und Frantzosisch, und jetzo auff das neuw in Teutsche Spraach mit fleiss iibersetzt (by T. sub Cruce), Strassburg, 1624. 46 Aethiopische Liebes und Helden-Geschichte aus dem Griechischen iibersetzt durch M. Christian Wplhelm Agricola, Jena, 1750. 47 Theagenes und Chariclea, eine Aethiopische

Geschichte in zehn Biichern, aus den Griechischen des Heliodorus iibersetzt (by J. N. Meinhard), Leipzig, 1767.
48 Historia Etiopica de los amores de Teagenes y Cariclea. Anadida la vida del autor, y una tabla de sentencias, etc. (edited by P. P. Bogia). A. Martin, Madrid, 1615. 49 Historia de Heliodoro delle cose Ethiopiche.

Nella quale fra diversi, compassionevoli avenimenti di due amanti, si contengono abbattimenti, descrittioni de paesi e molte altre cose, tradotta dalla lingua Greca nella Thoscana da L. Ghini, Vinegia, 1556.
50 lb., Gioliti, Venezia, 1587. 51 lb., Vinegia, 1611. 52 Historia Ethiopica... trasladada de Frances en vulgar Castellano por un segreto amigo de su patria F. de Mena y corrigida según el Griego por el mismo, Anvers, 1554. 53 La nueva Cariclea, ó nueva traducción de la novela de Theagenes y Chariclea, que con titulo de Historia Etiopia escrivió. .. Heliodoro translated by F. M. de Castillejo, Madrid, 1722. 54 La historia de los dos leales amantes Theagenes y Chariclea. Trasladada agora de nuevo de Latin en Romance por Ferñado de

Mena, Alcalá de Henares, 1587.

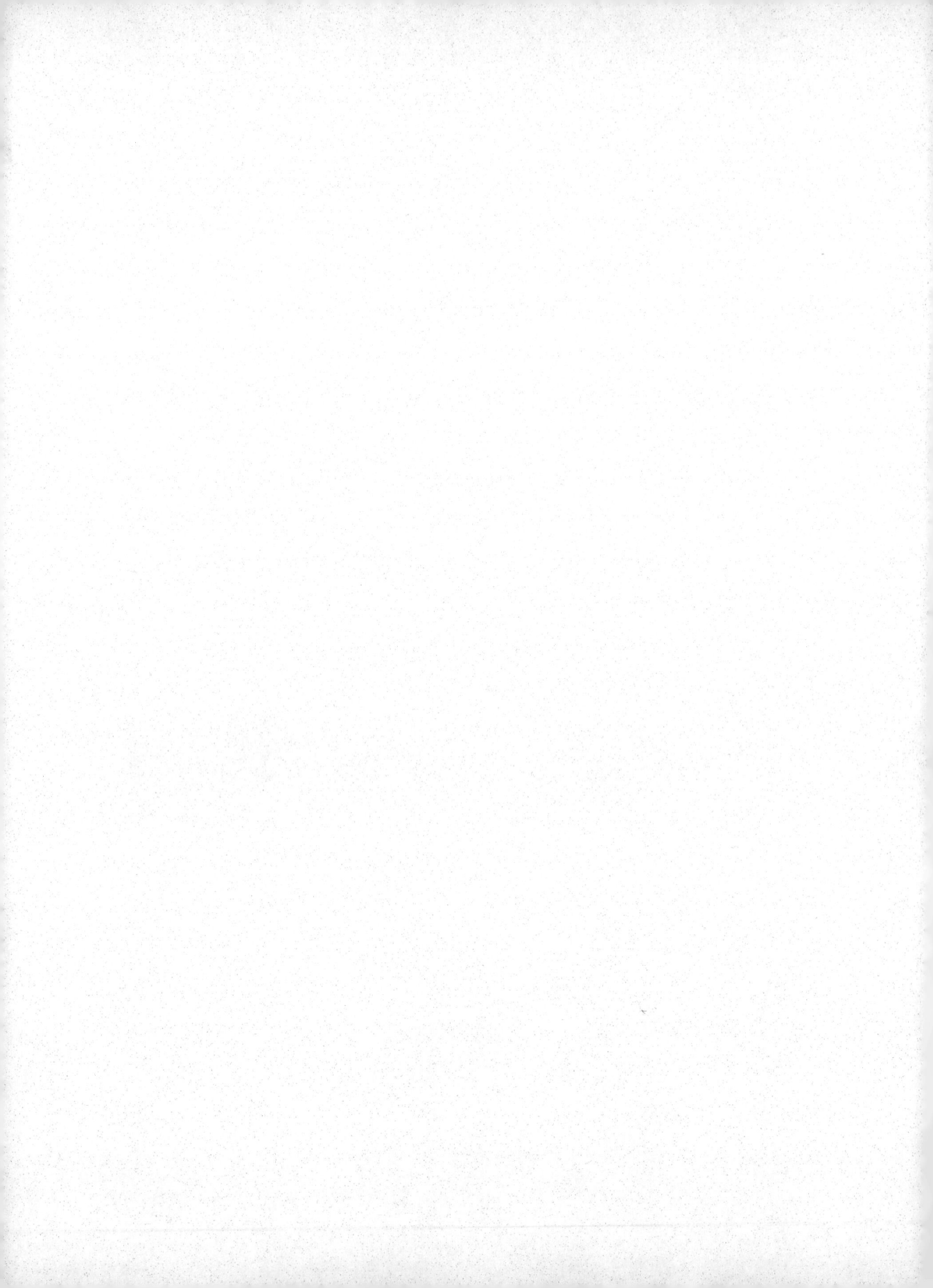

CPSIA information can be obtained
at www.ICGtesting.com
Printed in the USA
BVOW04s2031221217
503317BV00054B/1216/P